The Crystal Healing Guide for Beginners

Learn the Power and Rituals to Clean, Clear, and Activate Your Heart, Mind, and Soul

Table of Contents

Introduction 3
Chapter One: What Are Crystals? How Are They Formed? 8
    How to Find the Right Crystals 12
Chapter Two: Making Crystals Work for You........................14
    How Do Crystals Work? 14
    Crystals and the Law of Attraction......................................16
    Increasing the Effectiveness of Crystals.............................19
Chapter Three: Why Do Crystals Work?................................21
    Ways of Using Healing Crystals 23
Chapter Four: Benefits of Crystals.. 26
Chapter Five: Crystal Cleansing.. 32
Chapter Six: Types of Crystals and its Healing Properties or Characteristics 39
Chapter Seven: Intention Setting With Crystals 63
    What is Intention?.. 63
    The Basics of Intention Setting 65
    Meditating with Crystals 71
Chapter Eight: Simple and Effective Ways to Use Crystals... 76
    How Can I Work with Crystals? 81
Chapter Nine: Using Crystals with the 7 Laws of Attractions 84
Chapter Ten: Crystal Rituals for Protecting Your Energy 89
Chapter Eleven: Quick Crystal Rituals 98
    Cultivating Head to Toe Chakra Healing with Crystals ... 105
Chapter Twelve: Crystals and Gemstones for the 7 Chakras.. 108
Conclusion 113

Introduction

Healing crystals leverage our planet's life offering elements. These semi-precious stones harness the energy of the sea, sun, moon, and other powerful natural components while connecting us with the earth. We feel one with the earth and its surrounding potent energy through the power of crystals. People often wonder about the healing powers and curative benefits of crystals. Will it work for you? It depends on your own faith and how open you are to the entire experience of working with crystals. Anything you do with an open and accepting heart has the power to create miracles, and it's no different with crystals. These stones are capable of bringing about a transformation in your energy through the vibration influence of forces in and around the earth. Once you embark on the journey of healing through crystals, you'll realize how fulfilling, intriguing, and rewarding it can be. Keep your beliefs strong and heart open to enjoy the munificent benefits of the earth's healing powers. Yes, crystals will literally rock your world when you understand how to use them.

This book is intended to help people who have absolutely no or some experience with crystals, and desire to utilize their healing power for manifesting intentions and everything they wish to create in their life. The book aims at equipping you with all the information and knowledge necessary to embark on a spiritual journey. Crystals are capable of holding our intention and reminding us of our connection with nature of Mother Earth. They may help form, create, transform, and align our energies to accomplish the life of our dreams.

A purposeful and thoughtful intention is the beginning point of making crystals work for you since precise and meaningful intentions entering our everyday thought patterns become an integral part of its energy vibrations. Our thoughts have energy vibrations that are released into the universe. This energy becomes a vital component of a part of earth we hold with us (in the form of crystals) to help us manifest our desires and experience a sense of connection with the earth. When we set a clear and specific intention, the universe responds with a matching frequency. The entire universe holds energy vibrations (including our thoughts) that are latching on to matching other energy frequencies to create our life or reality. Thus, a crystal is a real, solid, tangible object that connects us with the earth with their power vibrations. We continue to connect with the intention crystal's energies by placing them on our skin and within our surroundings. Every thought, emotion, and intention energy vibration is picked up by the crystals, which then go on to multiply the positive vibrations we are nurturing. Crystals primarily work because they hold our intention and remind us of our powerful connection with the earth.

Crystals are effective because they have been present on the earth's surface since the onset of time. A majority of ancient cultures and civilizations have harnessed the power of crystals as healing and protective talismans. Even today, crystals are known to be one of the widest used peace offerings, ritual objects, and jewelry material. In the present era, quartz comprises 12 percent of our planet's crust. It is utilized in almost every form of technology including watches, electronics, data storage, and others.

Crystals communicate via computer chips, which mean it is possible to transform its vibrational energy in multiple ways.

With their strong link to the earth and life offering elements, crystals are considered universally healing.

Albert Einstein aptly stated that everything around within and around is energy. Much like sound energy or waves, our thoughts attract corresponding energy or vibrations, which become our reality. Thus everything that we've manifested in our life is a result of energy our thoughts have emitted into the universe. The vibrations of our thoughts create a matching energy response that becomes our reality. This is the essence of the Law of Attraction. Positive thoughts therefore release a positive energy frequency into the field of the universe and help us manifest positive things in our life. Similarly, negative thoughts attract more negative actions and occurrences in our life. When we believe crystals possess healing powers, the positive crystal vibrations increase the magnitude of our positive thoughts.

At each point in time, we have the power to choose what thoughts we focus our energies on. Healing crystals teach us to calm our mind and connect with the earth's healing vibrations and forces. The most important lessons crystals teach us is the power of patience. Much like these crystals take time to form, evolve, and transform, it takes time to work with their healing power. As we grow, develop, and learn, crystals serve as a tangible reminder about gratitude for the natural wealth that Mother Nature offers us.

Have you heard Law of Attraction and manifestation experts refer to the gratitude rock? What is this gratitude rock? It is a rock that acts as a tangible, physical representation for everything that we are grateful for in our life. It is a physical form of abundance bestowed on us by the earth and universal forces. Imagine if your positive energy and thankfulness can instill positive vibrations in a simple rock, how effective it will be when it comes to crystals. It is the same principle. These crystals pretty much work and align with our energy to shower the earth's abundant benefits. In essence, crystals are nothing but beautiful looking stones created as a result of geological activity in the earth's surface.

When we express gratitude towards the rock or stone by keeping it in our bag, purse, or wallet all the time, we are in essence thanking the earth's magnificent resources or the universe for everything that it has bestowed upon us, thus amplifying the positive energy of creating or attracting more of these blessings in our life. The positive energy in these crystals or rocks makes it easy to activate our manifesting energy.

A majority of what we refer to as crystals or healing stones are minerals that occur in varied forms. While certain stones result from a single mineral, others are formed by multiple mineral combinations. A few of these crystals based on their clarity, hardness, and color are termed gemstones (since they are rare and therefore precious).

One of the original pieces of scientific evidence connected to the benefits of crystals is IMB scientist Marcel Vogel's work. While observing crystals increase in size under a microscope, Vogel noted that their form changed according to his thoughts. Thus, he concluded that these energy vibrations are a direct result of the perpetual formation and destruction of the crystal's molecular bonds. The scientist also went on to test quartz crystal's metaphysical powers to conclude that rocks are capable of storing emotions and thoughts pretty much like how earlier tapes used magnetic energy for sound recording.

Holding crystals or placing them near our skin or energy field is known to facilitate physical, psychological, and spiritual healing. This happens because the crystal's energy positively interacts with our body or energy field to discard stress and negativity while facilitating greater positivity, enhanced focus, and creativity.

The reason crystals may work positively for you is because they give you a physical or tangible energy form to work with. Our mind is perhaps the most powerful force in the universe. It can help us set and manifest intentions by releasing the right vibrations into the universe. Crystals give a tangible form to that energy exchange. It represents the energy exchange between us and the earth to help manifest our deepest desires.

Chapter One: What Are Crystals? How Are They Formed?

Most gemstones or crystals occur naturally as minerals formed within the surface of the earth. Crystals are special types of solid matter where molecules come together in a repetitive pattern. This pattern causes the material to create all types of stunning and unique shapes. They are often formed in nature when liquids come together and solidify in an attempt to gather more stability. This happens in a repetitive pattern, which leads to the formation of beautiful looking crystals. When liquid rock known as magma cools gradually, it may lead to the formation of crystals.

A crystal is nothing but a solid substance with atoms aligned in repetitive crystal systems. There are seven kinds of crystal systems, with each resulting from a distinct physical geometric pattern. A common characteristic across all crystals is that they have atoms that are tightly arranged and aligned in lattice type patterns. Any mineral that has atoms aligned or arranged in one such pattern qualifies as crystalline or crystal.

The seven types of crystalline are cubic, orthorhombic, triclinic, trigonal, tetragonal, monoclinic, and hexagonal. To find a crystal in any of these shapes needs specific circumstances. These crystalline shapes can be created only if there are sufficient space and factors such as chemicals, pressure, heat, space, and time. A majority of times, these ideal conditions aren't available. In the absence of this, crystals are formed in other ways. Aggregates are clusters of small crystal formations that come together. Though these aggregates may appear amorphous, they are created out of several thousand microscopic crystals. One of the most unique characteristics of crystals is that they have extremely flat surfaces known as facets. They can assume a variety of shapes based on the atomic and molecular reaction that goes into the formation of the crystal. How to pick the right crystal? Healing and intention setting crystals have been used since times immemorial, and a plethora of information and experiences related to it have been handed down from generation to generation. Once you obtain more information about crystals, use your sense of connection and intuition to pick the right healing crystals for embarking on a fulfilling spiritual journey. We invariably experience a strong sense of connection with some crystals. Crystal professionals often reiterate how we don't choose crystals, they choose us! Using your intuition and tuning in to your inner psychic faculties is the best way to pick a crystal that is right for you. Stroll around a room packed with crystals and observe the ones that stand out. What attracts you to a particular crystal? Is it the resplendent color, shape, or pattern? Is it something powerful and unexplainable that attracts you to the crystal? Every crystal (much like every person) holds a unique energy vibration. This energy vibration is effective when it comes to cleansing blockages and eliminating negative energy.

Do you want to understand how crystals are formed with a simple DIY exercise? It explains the formation, creation, and composition of crystals in a highly simple yet effective manner.

Here's a DIY to make your own crystals so you understand the process of crystallization more effectively. The easiest method involves making sugar to create rock candy. Use a large pot of water and stir a large quantity of sugar into it. When you notice sugar settling at the bottom and there's no room to add more, it has reached saturation point. The water absorbs as much sugar as it can. This is known as supersaturation.

Bring the water to boil. While boiling, the intensity of saturation changes. The solution is not supersaturated anymore. You can keep adding more sugar. Again, add more sugar until you arrive at the supersaturation level again. Take your pot off the stove. Water will now slowly cool to room temperature. Now, the quantity of sugar it is capable of holding will go back to the previous level. The extra sugar will come to a solution. As it gradually comes to form a solution, sugar crystallizes.

Throw in a string inside the sugar solution for the crystals to climb on. Use a weight at string bottom to keep it erect. Though the process isn't quick enough to be observed unaided, you will notice a change in the crystals every few minutes. When the solution comes to room temperature, these sugar crystals will completely wrap around the string. The water will become supersaturated again.

This basic exercise introduced us to the four out of the five components that are needed for mineral crystallization. These are temperature, time, pressure, and space. Within the earth's surface, the crystal ingredients are more intricate, innumerable, and complex than our DIY sugar solution. They contain a variety of minerals. At a high temperature, the solution may contain several minerals in suspension. When the temperature plunged, the quantity of solid ingredients it is capable of holding in suspension also reduced. When this occurs, crystals are formed. There are a variety of minerals within the same solution that will all crystallize at varying temperatures. For instance, corundum may crystallize initially, followed by topaz and quartz, once the solution continues cooling.

Pressure has zero effect on the creation of rock candy though it takes an appropriate combination of temperature and pressure to crystallize minerals. Gems that are crystallized underground generally need intensely high temperatures and pressures. Space and time are fairly clear. The right proportion of heat, pressure, and natural materials must sustain for the minerals to crystallize. They need space to grow. Obviously, a 5 cm crystal can't grow in a 5mm space cavity.

Let us consider the conditions that are present below the earth's surface that leads to crystallization and gem formation.

The earth's crust ranges from 3 miles density under the ocean bed to 25 miles below land continents. There is a mantle below the crust, around 1,900 miles thick. This mantle comprises 83 percent of the planet's volume. It is comprised of molten rock known as magma. In a rare occurrence when it comes to the surface, it is termed as lava. The mantle's heat is at its peak near the epicenter of the earth, while it is (mantle) kept in constant motion by heat currents.

The earth's crust and mantle combine in a tough zone with increased pressures and temperatures. Innumerable plates that form the crust float on the liquefied mantle. As they combine, some are thrown down while others go up the mountains. Magma is also forever in motion. Its pressure, intensity, and movement create fracturing at the bottom of the earth's crust. As a consequence of this activity, rocks break away from the crust and combine with the liquid magma. A majority of these rocks melt, thereby altering the magma's chemical composition. Some tinier particles become a part of forthcoming gems.

The lower surface of the crust is increasingly fractured and comprises innumerable cavities. Liquids flowing from the magma pass through these fractures, which have near perfect conditions for crystal growth. Chemical rich liquids provide the required ingredients, while cavities give crystals space for growth. The temperature and pressure in this zone are high. As this liquid flows through the earth's crust, it cools down sufficiently to crystallize. Time is now the only component that's remaining.

How to Find the Right Crystals

You may not find your perfect crystal immediately, and shouldn't push yourself into finding one too. It is a disciplined and dedicated practice (much like any alternate wellness practice). Choosing the right crystal takes time and patience. Our mind should be calm. Our body's mental and physical balance may need to be realigned. One of the best techniques for picking the right crystal is to hold it in your hand for a while to determine its impact on your being. How do you feel when you hold the crystal in your hand? Are there sudden warm and cold sensations in the body? Do you feel a deep sense of calmness and serenity? Are there increased pulsations? These may be indicators that the rock is ideal for your healing requirements.

Crystals also help realign your energies to cope with a particularly challenging life situation. For instance, Fluorite is effective for clearing psychological and mental confusion if you are finding it tough to concentrate. Citrine can help attract material abundance and prosperity in your life since it helps channelize powerful positive energy vibrations of the sun. Similarly, carnelian is effective for getting the creative juices going.

If you find it challenging to let go of old ideas that no longer serve a purpose in your life, Black Tourmaline can be a highly potent gemstone for releasing negative and unwanted patterns that turned into destructive habits. It helps eliminate all the negative energy accumulated within your body and the surrounding energy field. It is also known to be a protection talisman and is especially effective for people who quickly pick up negative energy released by other people (empaths and sensitive people). Likewise, hematite is wonderful for dodging the negative mood and energies for other people by helping us reestablish a connection between our spirit and the earth's energy.

Chapter Two: Making Crystals Work for You

How Do Crystals Work?

Crystals have been utilized since ancient times as a powerful healing source, erstwhile cultures and civilizations across the world have harnessed the power of these stones when it comes to aligning, clearing, balancing, and transforming energy, physical, and emotional health and spirit. Several ancient cultures, including the Mayans and Egyptians, have utilized the power of crystals to bring about physical, mental, and spiritual well-being. These crystals often decorated the jewelry, architecture, and bodies of ancient Egyptians and Mayans.

Although the ancient cultures were well-versed with the spiritual, mental, and physical healing properties of crystals, it remained surprisingly unknown to the modern millennial. Thankfully, there has been a resurgence of interest in crystals and a new found enthusiasm in using their healing properties. People are now using the healing properties of crystals beyond the regular pharmaceuticals.

Research in the field of atoms has consistently revealed that our entire universe is made of energy. Even what we know as solid matter such as furniture, hair, or pencil are merely energy vibrations at their most basic level. They are all vibrating energies. Similarly, healing crystals, as well as our body cells, hold energy.

Scientists have discovered different ways to utilize energy held in crystals for timekeeping (think small quartz crystals in watches) as well as channelizing other electronic components such as computers and smartphones. Whether you've figured it out or not, energetic properties held within crystals are widely utilized in modern technology.

Pretty much like magnets use energy for attracting or repelling energy, healing stones attract and repel energies. When specific crystals are placed on certain body parts, it transforms our energy. Everything from our vibrations to pulses to moves change according to the crystal's properties and energetic attributes.

Healing crystals can be used to heal a variety of physical and mental conditions such as anxiety, migraines, stress, and more. They are also known to amplify the effect of meditation (when used regularly with meditation practices), align our body's seven chakras, and lower trace states in the right circumstances. There is just no limit to harnessing the power of crystals for bringing about overall healing through appropriate action.

If we desire to use the healing aspects of crystal for the mind, body, or spirit, there are three fundamental ways of transforming our energy and restoring balance.

Clearing – Crystals possess the ability to absorb or eliminate specific types of energy present in our body. It acts as a magnet that gathers metallic shavings to absorb unwanted and negative energies from our body.

Energizing – Healing crystals, as well as stones, can also infuse energy into your body, mind, and spirit by induction of resonant frequencies. The principle is similar to the generation of electricity, which works through conduction and transfer of energy into matter or an object. A crystal is capable of extracting energy from the wider quantum field and transferring it into your energy field to bring about more positive and constructive energy your way. This energy is without currents, though so you are safe!

Balancing – The universe is symmetrical in nature. Consider everything from the leaves on trees to our bodies. The earth's energy is aligned in a structured and mirrored pattern. At times, our energy is not effectively aligned, which leads to feel out of balance. Crystals can use their properties to attract, repel, and balance areas suffering from energetic disharmony.

Crystals and the Law of Attraction

If you are already using the powerful Law of Attraction in the form of visualizing, journaling, affirmations, and more to manifest your dream life, crystals will amplify the process. You are probably already on the path of living a happier and more meaningful life by setting the right goals and intentions. There are several creative and interesting ways to apply the Law of Attraction for manifesting your desires. Let us look at how healing crystals can be utilized in alignment with the Law of Attraction to activate your potential and set you on the dream life path.

The way to harness the power of crystals during visualizations or manifesting your goals is to simply hold them in your hand while you are practicing your Law of Attraction visualizations. Keep visualizing what you want in explicit details. Think about your goals as if they have already been fulfilled, and internalize the feelings and emotions of how you will you feel once your desires are manifested. When you think positive thoughts related to your desires, this energy is transmitted to the crystal.

The crystal does acts as an anchor for your positive thoughts and emotions.

Remember how we associate certain songs with feeling/emotions or memories of a specific point of time in our life? This is because the song acts as an anchor for those feelings, emotions, and memories. Similarly, when we visualize our desires in detail and experience the feelings and emotions felt while visualizing it, the crystal acts an anchor for these powerful positive feelings and emotions. Each time you are performing some action that is intended to take you closer to your goals, touch and feel your crystal. This will activate the same powerful and positive feelings you experience while practicing visualization, which in turn will help you attract matching vibrations. The simple act of touching your crystal will make you feel closer to your goals and more confident of accomplishing them.

Say, for instance, you want to attract more prosperity, money, and abundance. You visualize in great detail how life is like when you attract limitless prosperity and abundance. Hold a citrine in your hand while visualizing your prosperous life. Each time you go looking for a new job or business opportunity, sign a contract, negotiate a deal and so on, carry it with you in a bag or on your body. It will help you connect with same feelings and emotions that you experience during visualizations, and help you feel one with them to facilitate the manifestation process. Crystals become the carriers of your manifestation energy and help remind you of your goals, visions, and dream life images from time to time.

The one thing that crystals do is enhance our ability to attract more positive vibrations. When we hold crystals on our person or within our energy field, we are amplifying the power of our positive thoughts to attract even more of what we desire in life.

Boosting creativity

If you've always fancied writing a book, painting, or taking up a creative project, smoky quartz is your healing crystal. It is widely known to be associated with combating energy blocks (the writer's block too).

There are other stones too that have similar functions, which is why it is important to rerate the importance of choosing a stone that connects with you at an intuitive level. Keep either of these stones on your desk for tapping into your creativity and imagination and overcoming procrastination.

Attracting a new job or opportunities

Agate is known to be a bright and beautiful stone when it comes to staying brave and strong in the face of challenges. Similarly, tiger eye is a wealth stone, while the citrine eye is also effective for attracting abundance, money, and prosperity. Agate is especially helpful for people looking for a promotion or raise.

People who have an interview or important presentation lined up can harness the power of septarian, which is a popular healing stone intended to increase communication skills. Garnet is popular for enabling achievement and accolades at work. These crystals can be safely placed in a bag or your clothes in such a way that they are not visible. Feeling the power of the stone will instantly draw you to your visualizations of fulfilling your goals or manifesting your dream life.

Increasing the Effectiveness of Crystals

Visualize them working

The absence of any clear scientific evidence that crystals impact our mind and body, we only have our thought energies to work with. Of course, it has been determined that crystals like quartz are capable of holding and transmitting a great deal of information, which means crystals communicate and exchange energies. While using your crystal, the most important factor is faith or belief. You must operate from a space of belief. There must be faith that the crystal you hold on your hand or wear on your being works for you. You must believe that it has the energies to bring about a balance in your body, mind, and spirit. The placebo effect becomes a moot point in the absence of clear beliefs. Crystals work when you believe they do. Place crystals strategically on your body parts while concentrating on their healing characteristics. Place rose quartz over your heart and visualize it carrying you away from sadness and loneliness. Similarly, if you find it challenging to face an audience or be a confident public speaker, put a kyanite blue crystal near your throat and visualize it releasing your fears and inability to speak the truth.

Focus on the chakras

Another popular way to utilize crystals is to assemble the stones in alignment with the body's seven chakras or energy centers. While meditating, we can place a crystal just under our stomach to activate the sacral chakra, closely connected with sexuality and creativity. Again, if you are looking for more clarity, wisdom, and awakening on a matter, you can place the crystal between your eyebrow, the position of the anja chakra or third eye (also as the focal point of our intuition).

Carry them around

Some people like to have a crystal in their bag, pocket, or as a piece of jewelry all the time. It instills greater confidence and faith in them throughout the day, especially when they are heading for an important task. The key is to keep touching and feeling the crystal in your pocket, handbag, or body. Put your hand in your handbag to remind yourself that you have a crystal that is passing on its magnificent energies to you. Crystals can also be planted around the house to make you feel more safe, secure, grounded, and balanced. It can also be placed next to revered objects to enhance the positive vibrations of a space. For instance, it can be used to boost the positive energies in a prayer, meditation, healing, or tarot card reading room. You may have your own reading, yoga, or pampering zone in the house, where these crystals can be used to infuse greater positivity. There are several ways to use the healing powers of crystals. It actually depends on the methods and ways you connect with at a deeper level, since at the end of the day, this is alternate healing that relies primarily on intuition and connection at deeper, more profound levels.

Chapter Three: Why Do Crystals Work?

Crystals possess energy properties that work with our energy systems to affect our body, mind, and spirit. They are also known to be effective in specific challenges and instances Say, things aren't going great where your job/money is concerned or you aren't having a good run in your romance/love life, crystals enthusiasts believe crystals can help restore a sense of balance within your mind and body to help resolve the challenging situation. *The Sun* carried a report a few years ago about how Adele misplaced her crystals just before her Grammy act, which led to a series of technical issues during the performance. There are plenty of examples of how crystals have positively impacted people's lives and how its energies have helped transform or balance our energies, though there is no conclusive scientific evidence to prove the same, much like many other alternative healing methods. The effectiveness of crystals is largely dependent on your faith alone. This faith generates a sort of energy that attracts similar energy vibrations from the earth in the form of crystals.

For example, let us say you use citrine or the money/prosperity stone for attracting more wealth. This involves you expressing gratitude for what you already have and activating power 'money thoughts.' Since our thoughts possess energy, we transmit powerful abundance and prosperity thought vibrations that are absorbed by the crystal. Thus, it responds in a similar frequency by bringing to our notice opportunities to manifest these desires. Faith in the stone realigns thoughts and energies, which in turn helps us accomplish what our heart truly desires.

While this is pop culture and makes for interesting trivia, fact remains that crystals are much sought after when it comes to their healing properties. Though there is no clear scientific evidence point to the fact that crystals impact our body or brain. However, our thoughts are what activate the placebo effect and power of crystals. As discussed earlier, our thoughts have powerful energy vibrations. This energy vibration exchange that happens between our being and the crystals helps in setting intentions and activating our potential.

Healing crystals are powerful, magical entities that are alive with energy. There is a clear reason human beings have harnessed the healing benefits of these crystals since the onset of time. They are known to help live a more buzzing, aligned, and balanced life when utilized well and with the required reverence. Much like all other objects we own, crystals should be deeply respected for them to work. Though crystals have gained tremendous popularity in the last few years, it is important to use them sustainably with the right intention. One must use these gifts from Mother Earth with a conscious and mindful intention without overtly harvesting these gifts from the planet. Ensure you know the origins and mining place of the crystals. This is integral to the process and often overlooked. Remember, your crystals hold energy. Their origin and the mining activity they were subjected to create their energies. Right from the time they are extracted to when they are placed in your hands, they are accumulating the energy of every process. Make these relevant and meaningful for your purpose!

Ways of Using Healing Crystals

There are several thousand types of healing crystals in the world and based on your intuition and intention, you can pick the one that best resonates with your spirit. They hold a surprisingly large amount of healing properties, some of which may not even be known yet. There is a lot of untapped energy and potential in these crystals that you can harness for your own well-being and development. Before you go into discovering your perfect crystal, here are some ways to use these miracle objects for healing yourself.

Wearing healing crystals – Since crystals and gemstones absorb, repel, and transfer energy, wearing specific healing crystals can help balance our energy field through the day. These healing crystals are like vitamins for the body that nourish and infuse it with energy throughout the day. Wear your crystals in the morning or place them in your pocket for elevating your energy levels.

Place crystals on a body part – This is stone laying or placing crystals on the part of your body which you are seeking to heal through the application of crystal energy. It is an excellent way to harness the healing properties of a crystal. For instance, let us say you have a terrible backache. You may lay on your back quietly while placing a crystal on the pain region. This will help alleviate the pain and leave you feeling more energized. Again, if you have a persistent headache, placing a quartz crystal on the pain spot may leave it feeling less troublesome and more healed.

Meditate with crystals – Healing crystals often date back millions of years, which mean they hold plenty of historical energies and information. Did you know that a quartz crystal can hold an amount of data equivalent to 22,000 iPhones?

Plus, this information doesn't degrade with time. By meditating and quietly contemplating with crystals, you can train your mind to cut the chatter during meditation. This makes you more intuitively receptive to multiple life-transforming insights. Imagine, a simple act of holding a piece of energy in your hand can help bring a sense of calmness and tranquility within your mind, body, and spirit.

Use a crystal grid – Another popular way of using crystals for healing is to lay a crystal grid. You can lay out particular types of stones and crystals in a predetermined structure. These structures are created to transfer and receive energy. A crystal grid is a more ancient healing method and it may take a while to learn various types of grids for a beginner. However, mastering crystal grids may be worth it because it's known to be a highly potent practice.

Sleep with crystal – We know how powerful our subconscious mind is. When fed with the right energies and ideas, it is capable of creating near impossible things. While we are asleep, our conscious mind is resting. This is when our subconscious mind is most active. It is a great time for healing and learning at a fast pace. Our subconscious mind absorbs everything that's fed into it and believes it to be our truth. This is why life coaches, affirmation experts, and manifestation gurus recommend practicing visualization just before going to bed.

Allow crystals to work their magic while you are sleeping to eliminate any potential hurdles from your path that your conscious mind may perceive with fear or uncertainty. Place the crystal under your pillow or on a bedside table to gauge its energies or effects on your dreams, thoughts, and feelings. Check how you feel when you awaken in the morning. Are there any changes in the way you think, feel, and dream? Give yourself some time to notice these changes or a shift in your subconscious vibrations.

Circulate them around the body – Crystals do not have to stay in one place to reveal their effectiveness. At times, it is more effective to move them around the body to maximize their healing powers. Try utilizing a crystal wand to ward off negative energy fields from top to bottom. Start to with your head and go right up to the toe. Bear in mind that our energy field extends to about 3 feet around us. This means you shouldn't shy away from crystal healing the entire aura surrounding you.

Place them in your vehicle or home – Crystals are magnificent for offering protection or empowering an intention. For instance, you can place crystals in your car to ward off negative energy from robberies and accidents. This can be done by placing the appropriate intentions into your crystals and them placing them in these specific places. They can be used in a similar manner in your entire house or a specific room. Set the energy or intention for a room by using the right crystals. For example, rose quartz can be left in the bedroom to attract romantic energy.

Chapter Four: Benefits of Crystals

For several hundred years, people have harnessed the power of crystals to eliminate our mental, spiritual, and physical energy blockages. As they originate from our planet, crystals help us connect with the healing energy of Mother Earth. This makes us feel calmer, positively energized, and balanced. It is a myth that one has to be spiritually inclined to enjoy the benefits of crystals. One can make the most of crystal's energies even without being overtly spiritual or mystically inclined. Each crystal provides a unique property that can help heal, balance, energize, and charge several aspects of one's life.

Crystals have been recognized since the onset of civilization to be prized not only for their beauty but also their spiritual, balancing, and healing powers. These power elements have been used by shamans, priests, and Wicca experts for their unique characteristics. It is widely known that crystals vibrate on a similar pitch as humans. The resonance or interaction between crystals and humans helps ward off negative vibrations of health and other areas that need a boost.

There are crystals to help us lead a well-rounded love life, crystals that can help us attract greater wealth, crystals to help enhance our professional life, and crystals that help release negative emotions such as rage, sadness, self-doubt, and more.

Boosting energy

If you are running low on energy, an appropriate crystal won't just offer you an energy boost but also enhance your drive, excitement, and enthusiasm while overcoming lethargy and sending negative thoughts down the drain. In ancient times, bloodstone was believed to have been worn as an amulet for blood purification and for along the blood to flow smoothly. Red stones and crystals in general are known to stimulate or energize. A ruby crystal, for instance, is a classic example of a red crystal that provides balance and energy.

Optimizing health and clearing the mind

A quartz crystal made of silica is perhaps the most thriving and prosperous elements on earth. It touches our energy and skin, which bestows us with high healing, energy, and heath. Its vibrations are known to be powerful for one's health. It impacts the body on a cellular level. Older civilizations utilized crystal for bringing about a sense of balance in the body and clarity in the mind. This is a power-packed crystal that helps raise our body's vibrations while also inducing greater mental clarity. There are other stones too that are known to have a powerful effect on the body and help a person release unexpressed emotions.

Eliminate unproductively and creativity blocks

Crystals can help a person feel unstuck if they feel stuck, uninspired, and burned out. An orange crystal such as carnelian is wonderful for instilling a sense of warmth. The dazzling color is known to trigger our passions so that we can move ahead with them and accomplish our goals by enhancing our enthusiasm, excitement, and motivation. It is known as an action stone since at a physical level, the crystal helps facilitate vitality by enhancing the absorption of both minerals and vitamins while ensuring that our blood flows smoothly into our body's tissues and organs.

Relief against anxiety and stress

In today's contemporary and chaos filled world, we tend to suffer from increasing stress and anxiety. Almost 1 out of every 5 Americans suffers from some type of anxiety disorder. Crystals can come to our rescue here too. There are several crystals that provide relief, including amethyst that is known not just to ward off anxiety and stress but also keep at bay anger, mood swings, depression, and fear. If you are a highly sensitive person or empath, wearing a suitable crystal will help you repel your negative energy while drawing more positive energy. Place the crystal under your pillow at night to help cope with nightmares.

People suffering from muscle stress can use celestite on the affected region for relief. Celestite's name originates from the Latin term caleestis that literally celestial. All a person has to do is keep gazing at it. It is known to induce sense happiness, contentment, and peace. For those having trouble sleeping due to anxiety, depression, and stress, keep this crystal under your pillow or place it on a nightstand adjacent to your bed for a more relaxed and peaceful sleep.

Release resentment and anger

If you are having trouble forgiving yourself or another person, or are coping with feelings of guilt, shame, and regret, crystals can help cleanse and recharge your energies. They can help us break barriers such as resentment, anger, guilt, and sadness to practice more forgiveness. There are several crystals such as rhodonite that can be used for combating such a scenario that has brought sadness, depression, and anger to help us release it with compassion, positive energy, and love. If you've dealt with major trauma, use the power of malachite to release it by holding in your hand while meditating. Visualize the person you desire to forgive by offering them these crystals as a gesture of forgiveness and later view it flying away. This is a wonderful way to heal a pained heart with crystals or to release painful childhood memories.

Enhancing our career

Crystals help enhance our career in several ways to help us accomplish greater success, wealth, self-development, and prosperity. If you find it challenging to work on a project and experiencing blockages at each turn, place a bloodstone as a paperweight on your work desk. It is known to remove roadblocks that come in the path of our success. This is known to be the stone of courage and helps you stand up to people who may be trying to intimidate you in addition to relieving pressure if you feel pressurized to accomplish unrealistic goals.

Utilize obsidian to ascertain that things go efficiently, whether you are in the process of finalizing a multi-million dollar deal or organizing an office Christmas party. It is a highly powerful defense system that helps us combat against powerful forces. It helps us use all our strength and power while enhancing self-confidence, which demonstrates that you are unafraid to take on big challenges. For those starting a new assignment, job and contract position, serpentine is great for dealing with changes related to the new assignment.

Attracting wealth, abundance, and prosperity

Crystals can assist us in attracting abundance, wealth, and prosperity. For those who have the habit of spending excessively, place citrine in your wallet or handbag. Citrine is known as a businessman or merchant's stone. It can also help those who run their own business. Place it in the cash register to ensure you attract more profits. Malachite is a stunning stone that is known to enhance a person's business prospects and chances of profits. It is great to draw this energy when you are making an important financial decision/deal or interviewing for your dream job. It can help by shielding your energies from unscrupulous people and attract more helpful people.

Peridot is a green crystal that resembles an emerald. It represents ancestral wealth and affluence. If you are grabbling with debt, ensure you keep this stone with you all the time. Tiger's eye can be valuable too. It is known to draw greater abundance, enhance your patience, and improve your money-making potential. It helps us save more money and take advantage of optimal opportunities by opening up your energy. It also helps increase optimism, confidence, and self-worth. By allowing your mind and energy field to open up, you are able to view innumerable opportunities that are everywhere around you draw infinite abundance.

Protection against EMF

Electronic devices such as laptops, smartphones, and microwaves radiate an electronic field. It is not possible to avoid these emissions as they are everywhere around us and have several unfortunate harmful effects on our physical and mental health. Shungite can be used as a powerful energy shield against EMF as it assists in absorbing bad energies, pollutants, and toxic substances. Place shungite near your electronic devices while you are working or wear it on your body as a protective shield.

Building love

Rose quartz is known to be a crystal associated with unconditional love. The pink crystal is believed to open as well as heal our heart energy. It radiates vibrations of kindness, beauty, compassion, and love. It helps nurture and support our spirit while allowing us to experience the universe's powerful energy and love. It will not just attract true love into our life but also encourages us to love yourself. If you are hurting from old wounds, it helps heal them. If you are carrying emotional baggage from previous relationships, it helps offer forgiveness to past lovers, while helping you release any leftover emotional baggage so that we are ready for love again.

Also, if you are single and seeking the perfect match, placing two rose quartz crystals adjacent to your bedside can be a good idea. Malachite is also a wonderful balancing stone that helps a person feel safer, self-assured, and secure, opening your heart to love in all its forms.

Chapter Five: Crystal Cleansing

Since we know by now that crystals accumulate and hold energy every step of the way throughout the process of their formation, it is important to start anew by cleansing them from any negative or damaging energy they may have attracted along from the time they have been mined until they reach your hands. Since crystals attract, absorb, and repel specific types of energies all the time, it is important to cleanse and charge them. Make a habit to keep your crystals positively energized from time to time to get the most of them. If you are using crystals for soaking negative energy, you may want to discard that negative energy before using the stone again. Think of these crystals as sponges. You use a sponge to clean dirty water. If you want to use the sponge again to clean a surface, you'll first need to get rid of the dirty water. Only once you clean out the dirty water can you ensure that the next thing you wipe with the sponge doesn't become dirty.

Where ever you purchase the stone from (online, local gemstone shop), the stone comes with energy it has absorbed or repelled over a period of time. Everyone who has touched the crystal before you has left their energy residues on the crystal. Before you begin using the crystals yourself, cleanse their energy and align it with your own vibrations.

Different healers and crystal experts follow different rituals for cleansing their crystals. While some work with the full moon for cleansing their crystals from previously held energies, others simply wash and wear them. We'll discuss a few methods here and you can pick the one that resonates with you. At the end of the day, these are your crystals. Make them work in the way you want them to. Cleanse them in a manner that makes you feel good about working with them.

The question that most beginner crystal users have is when should crystals ideally be charged? The answer is, as soon as you buy them or get them as gifts. Thereafter, every time you use it for healing purposes (wearing it, carrying it around, etc.), it needs to be charged.

If you are wearing these crystals as jewelry, cleanse them daily or twice a week, especially if they begin to look dull or lose their initial luster. All-purpose crystals that are utilized for healing our environment can be cleansed monthly. Since healing crystals are part of vibrational healing, they absorb and release energy. Hence, it is important to discard any negative energy build-up.

These stones can be charged based on their color, properties, and type. For instance, softer stones can be cleansed with moonlight rather than water. Irrespective of the method you use for cleansing your stones, ensure you are able to connect with it at a deeper level. Cleansing your crystal doesn't have to be a huge hassle. It can be performed with ease by setting the right intention.

Whether you purchase a new crystal for your collection or simply want more information about maintaining your existing stones, cleansing stones periodically is vital. The color, texture, characteristics, and feeling of the stone play an important role in our chakras and personality. Our vibrations are deeply attracted and attached to the stones we should wear. Hence, you must preserve, maintain, and care for your stones the way you look after yourself. The stones are an extension of your energy. Just the way you recharge, cleanse, and activate your energy, the crystals should also be cleansed and charged.

Irrespective of the stone you purchase, don't forget to read more about it in this book and cleanse it with a ritual that best matches its characteristics and purpose along with your intuition (go with a healing method or element that feels intuitively good to you).

Here are some elements for cleansing your crystals

Natural water

Natural water is one of the best neutralizers when it comes to directing negative energy stored within the stone back into the earth. Rinse your stones well and activate them with water by placing them under a natural water resource such as waterfalls or rain for about 5 minutes. If these resources aren't available, you can simply place them under a running faucet for 10-12 minutes. It is important to note that though there are no hard and fast rules when it comes to cleansing crystals, water has a strong physical force. It is best to cleanse only hard crystals such as amethyst, quartz, or turquoise using this method. The softer stones may have their properties washed away under the force of natural water. If you are using water for cleansing or charging your crystals, ensure the crystals aren't soluble before beginning.

Sun or Moonlight

This is the ultimate natural energy when it comes to charging your crystals. Want some yang or masculine energy for the crystal? Charge it with powerful solar energy. This will help balance the inherent yin energy it possesses from the earth throughout the process of its formation. For stones that are more prone to discoloration under the sun (amethyst, amber, or rose quartz), place them out for an hour during dawn.

Moonlight is a delicate and non-color changing method that is especially powerful during a full moon. There is a plethora of new moon cleansing and charging rituals used by healers, including the one mentioned in this chapter. Since the moon is at its fullest potential during a full moon, it enhances the stone's vibrations. Give your crystals a moon bath!

Fire

Fire or smoke can be utilized for cleansing your stones by quickly burning or smudging them. Direct fire instantly burns away negative energy in a matter of seconds with a candle. Smudge cleansing rituals can be performed with sage sticks, sandalwood or cedar incense, palo santo, and more. These are all known to ward off negativity. Hold your stone over the source of smoke (20-30 seconds) for cleansing it while your home also charges simultaneously.

Salt Water

Salt water baths are one of the most widespread and common ways for cleansing crystals. Throughout ancient civilizations and history, people have used the power of salt water for cleansing unwanted or negative energy absorbed by people, spaces, and objects. Using this technique, soak your crystals overnight in water by adding a pinch of sea salt to it. If you are fortunate enough to have access to the sea, you can take them back to nature and allow these crystals to sit in seawater in a mesh bag. Ensure they are rinsed in clean/clear water post the sea water cleansing to get rid of any residue. Be careful while using salt water for cleansing stone since salt can end up damaging some delicate stones like pyrite and hematite.

Earth

You can charge the crystals by taking them right where they belong. Bury the stone underground for an entire day. Allow the earth to soak all the negative and unwanted energies held within the stone so they are refreshed, reenergized, and cleansed. The earth is where they originate from and can act as a strong force for establishing your connection with nature as well as your crystals.

Meditation

Meditation is another widely used technique when it comes to cleansing crystals. Meditate for cleansing these crystals and gemstones.

Many people use it for balancing their own energies by breathing into the jewels. It is vital to state a clear intention so the crystal can be refueled once it has been cleansed. Once you master this crystal cleansing method, it will come naturally to you while offering you plenty of benefits. The calmness of your spirit will allow the stone to sterilize naturally. Again, you'll enjoy multiple benefits of meditation as well as crystal healing by practicing this method.

Ensure you don't practice this as a merely symbolic cleansing ritual. Practice in a relaxed, calm, and true meditative state. It is believed to be all the more effective if you meditate during the full moon period.

While we've discussed various elements that can be used for healing your crystals and making them even more powerful, here is a full-fledged full moon cleansing method that can be used for clearing your crystals off any negativity and unwanted vibrations.

Other crystals

Some crystals are extremely effective when it comes to cleansing or charging other crystals. Quartz and amethyst, in particular, possess the ability to regenerate charge and absorb energies emitting from other stones. One of the best stones when it comes to purifying negative energies held within a stone is selenite.

How does one cleanse crystals with the help of other crystals? To cleanse crystals using crystals, place them on selenite for a minimum of six hours (the longer the more effective). Selenite and clear quartz groups enhance the energy of your stones. They possess the ability to neutralize, absorb, cleanse, and recharge your stones with increased vibrations.

Full Moon Method

Here is a step by step full moon method for cleansing your crystals.

Wash your crystals well before you can begin. You can wash them in regular faucet water, no fancy stuff required. If you happen to live near a natural water resource such as a flowing stream or ocean, wash your crystals there.

Once washed, put them outdoors on a natural surface post sunset. It can also be placed on a window sill where direct moonlight reaches them. As you keep each crystal on a natural surface, name something that you desire to release from your life. You can name a single thing over and over with each crystal or have a different thing you want to let go off with each crystal. Limit it to below five things at a time to avoid lowering your energy vibrations. The full moon method is a supportive ritual that helps us seal what we are prepared to release.

Next, pull your crystals indoors the next morning and reenergize them with the sun's energy for a short while. Keep them through sunrise as a rule of the thumb and then get them inside.

Charge these crystals with powerful intentions. This is where the magic begins. Charging crystals with your own powerful energy and intention keeps these objects focused on a purpose. Once your crystals are charged, avoid letting others handle them unless you've charged it for someone else or clients. A crystal tends to absorb other people's energies, which means you don't want them to attract other energies before using them.

All your crystals can be charged together by visualizing them soaked in healing powers or energy. They can either be charged singularly or in clusters. It depends on you. There isn't a right or wrong way to charge crystals. It is your energy and crystals, let intuition lead you. Charge crystals to strengthen their healing powers even if you are using them on others!

Charge rose quartz to enhance your romantic relationship or smokey quartz to help you stay grounded while transitioning into a different season.

End the ritual. The cleansing and charging process can typically end with a prayer of gratitude directed to Mother Nature or the universe. Say thank you to Mother Earth for the way she supports us. Express gratitude for all the positive energies that the crystals bring you. Acknowledge all elements of nature that combine to offer their healing vibrations and remind you to stay focused on what your heart desires. Burn some cedar to attract even more positive energy and bring the ritual to a conclusion.

Chapter Six: Types of Crystals and its Healing Properties or Characteristics

There is a good reason crystals are growing in popularity across the world. These ancient minerals are wonderful spiritual tools that restore our faith and balance. There are innumerable minerals formed in Mother Earth's sacred womb. They rise to the surface only to transform into healing crystals that connect us to the earth while experiencing the miracles of cosmic energy and energy held within us.

Everything around us is made up of energy. Rocks, crystals, stones, and gems aren't any different. They comprise small crystals in precise molecular patterns that are perpetually in motion. These comprise tiny crystals in a very precise molecular pattern. Thus, each crystal emits an unusual vibration and unique energy field.

While some crystals are more all-encompassing in their application, others are known to possess specific metaphysical and physical healing attributes. Knowing more about their physical and metaphysical benefits will help you pick the right stone in alignment with your intention and desires.

We've briefly discussed in an earlier chapter how you must pick a crystal (or does the crystal pick you?) that you can connect with at a deeper level. These crystals must feel perfect on your being. No, there will be no bells ringing around you immediately and no instant magic happens. However, we intuitively and instinctively know when something feels right. When we feel better just holding the crystal in our hand or there are some notable physiological changes within us, the crystal may well be for us. Here is a beginner's guide to the different types of crystals along with their healing powers and characteristics. However, do not limit yourself to one crystal based on its properties, characteristics, and benefits. For instance, you may be struggling with your finances and may opt to carry a citrine. However, you may also want greater overall mental, physical, and spiritual balance, which means you may opt for a more all-encompassing stone such as selenite. Ask yourself these questions before picking the right crystal for you. What do I intend to accomplish by wearing these crystals? What do I want from them? What do I feel when I hold a particular crystal?

Different kinds of crystals carry different energies and healing characteristics. Though crystals inherently carry their own energy and healing properties, it is best to program your crystals with a particular intention. As one continues to work with a particular crystal, one connects even more intensely with one's main intention or purpose. Combine this with the magic of crystal to grow your intention and you've got a wonderful healing tool. Crystals can elevate our intention setting to a higher level. By programming our crystals with a clear intention, we can manifest our intentions and what we truly desire in life.

Pick the one that you are drawn to and that feels right to you. This is just a guideline to get you started in the right direction when it comes to selecting crystals. You may feel more drawn to one over others. At times, you may feel drawn to a stone based on its properties or characteristics. If they match your purpose, by all means, pick them up and infuse them with intention.

Selenite

This is known as the master mineral because it is the only healing crystal that is not required to be charged before using. It in fact used for cleansing and charging other crystals. It is safe to call it the big boss of all crystals. Selenite is the most abundant crystal, which is largely found in erstwhile salt lakes (evaporated) and oceans. It is predominantly found from Mexico or Brazil and further.

Selenite's metaphysical properties include its passageway to the highest level of human consciousness and everything that is infinite. It is closely connected with intuition, the universe, and spiritual guides. Selenite builds a close connection between the spirit world and earth while reinforcing where we have originated from along with where we are headed post this life.

Known for being a master crystal, there's practically nothing that selenite can't be used for when it comes to healing. Meditate on your intentions or a desired outcome while carrying the crystal. This can help activate your potential, while also bringing about healing, balance, and inner peace.

Aventurine

Aventurine is known as the stone of fortune and opportunity. It is known to amplify one's good luck as well as multiply abundance and prosperity. Planning to head for a job interview or a gambling trip? Carrying an aventurine may help. A variant of quartz stone, aventurine is known to draw luck and assist the person in successfully harnessing new opportunities available to them.

Aventurine is closely associated with our Heart Chakra. It creates an overall sense of well-being and emotional balance. Aventurine balances our emotional, physical, and mental faculties to build a sense of harmony within them. It creates a sense of balance among different aspects of our being.

Its physical healing properties include supporting the heart and blood circulation, while also facilitating energy circulation. One can help quicken recovery time from an ailment, surgery, or injury with the help of aventurine.

Citrine

Citrine is known to be a wealth and abundance stone. It is a type of quartz and comes in the hue of a dazzling golden yellow. Citrine is a dynamic golden shaded mirror that radiates the sun's luminosity and power. Similarly, citrine's energy represents optimism, prosperity, and creativity. This is one of the most powerful manifestation tools. When instilled with sunlight, it reflects our intentions, transforming our dreams or visions into reality.

Originating from the French word citron translating into lemon, citrine is known to be one of the most powerful and popular of all crystals. It is as sweet as it can be even though its name implies sour. It has a dazzling and sunny attitude that nourishes energy for growth. Citrine is known to energize our body's solar plexus chakra for radiating more power. It bestows the person who carries it around or wears it with the power-packed energy of the sun. Since it energizes our body's solar plexus chakra, Citrine is known to bring about greater power, confidence, patience, endurance, and centeredness. Instead of attracting negative energy, Citrine is known to clear it. The crystal makes room for light, positivity, energy, and happiness to enable our spirit to embrace several positive possibilities.

Carrying this stone to business meetings about finances, to the bank or while signing an important contract (negotiating a deal) can produce favorable circumstances for you. Many people prefer placing citrine at their work desk and look at it while working. Citrine helps attract wealth, prosperity, stability, and abundance in your life.

Owing to its natural autumn shades, Citrine is known to be the birthstone for those born in November. It is also known as the Merchant's Stone for its ability to attract wealth, abundance, and prosperity. While some refer to it as Merchant's stone, others call it the Success Stone for pretty much the same properties of attracting wealth and prosperity. If you are seeking financial prosperity, success in business ventures, wealth, greater abundance, Citrine is known to be one of the best manifestation facilitators. The stone is known to work closely with several other crystals such as golden labradorite and helidore for increasing your personal will and determination to accomplish a goal. It makes a person more perseverant, courageous, and strong-willed when it comes to manifesting their goals, especially ones related to business and wealth creation.

Success is a result of hard work, dedication, and efforts. However, at times, the hard work and focus are challenging to muster. You may be struggling to muster the fortitude for fulfilling your goals. Thus, manifesting a strong personal will allow you to chase your goals with the required tenacity. The right energies can help bolster the determination and effort that is required to fulfill a task or goal.

Citrine has plenty of other properties that are closely associated with the creative process. Whether in its natural form or heated, Citrine is known to activate the visualization and imagination of our body's third, sixth, and second chakras. It is believed to increase our mental clarity while allowing for free-flowing ideas and imagination. This is especially true when the crystal is utilized during the process of meditation and visualization. Citrine is extremely effective when it comes to strengthening our mental output, while also establishing clear objectives. There are several other stones that can be utilized in combination with Citrine to increase creativity and imagination. Some of these stones are Carnelian and Zincite.

Citrine is closely associated with our root, solar plexus, and sacral chakra. By linking with the sacral chakra, Citrine's healing properties can be used for facilitating an increase in sexual desire and fertility. The creation of both ideas and life can be abundant under Citrine's motivating powers. Citrine connects with our root chakra to facilitate the combining of our physical and emotional energy for raising it to a higher energy plane.

This is one chakra where maximum energy blocks in our body occur. Most people feel a sense of discomfort and misbalance when the root chakra is blocked. Citrine can be one of the most effective crystals when it comes to clearing the energy block within our root chakra.

Citrine can be used in a variety of ways. It can be kept in the bedroom to attract more light, power, sexual energy, and abundance into your intimacy space. Citrine can also be placed in your workspace for more creativity, imagination, and prosperity. It can infuse dazzling energy, focus, power, and security into children's bedrooms.

What are the benefits of meditating with Citrine? Meditating with Citrine brings about a sense of imagination, warmth, focus, and inspiration. Its positivity and power remain unparalleled. One of the best mantras to use while meditating with Citrine is "I am light and I enjoy spreading light."

This helps you radiate more energy and vibrancy while attracting greater energy into your mind, body, and soul for facilitating creativity. For activating Citrine's manifestation powers, write your intention on paper and put them under its points. You can also combine this ritual with a variety of stones to increase the manifestation goal.

When it comes to physical healing properties, citrine is known to smoothly facilitate our body's metabolic functions. It also helps in nausea, a feeling on tiredness, and digestion. Citrine is known to be highly effective when it comes to strengthening our nerve impulses and facilitating rapid functioning of the brain. Its radiance and luminescence are known to bestow sharpness to the brain.

Tourmaline

Tourmaline is a much sought after talisman for healing and protection. It is known to be an effective psychic shield for grounding a person's energy and fighting transmission of negative entities within your energy field. Tourmaline is commonly used by shamans, Wicca experts, magicians, and wizards across the world for its protective properties.

Where metaphysical healing properties are concerned, the black tourmaline is utilized for warding off damaging or negative energies. It also helps raise our positive vibrations, while leading us from the darkness of negative energy to the light of positive energy. Tourmaline is known to absorb dark, destructive energies while encouraging our spirit to stay strong and radiant during challenging dark times.

Tourmaline's physical healing characteristics include relief from joint pain and spine realignment. It can also be utilized for strengthening our immune system, adrenal glands, and heart. Tourmaline is also effective for alleviating stress and eliminating tension.

Fluorite

This crystal is possibly one of the most undervalued or underrated stones but also a powerful one. It is believed to literally suck negative energy and low energy vibrations from your body or given space to create greater space or room for light to enter and shine. Fluorite is found in several color variations and is known to be a profoundly magical crystal.

Fluorite's metaphysical healing properties include auric protection, lifting your energy vibration, transforming negative energy into positive energy, and calming a disturbed mind. Rainbow Fluorite is known to balance the mind and increase psychic connection to increase a person's intuitive powers.

Embracing fluorite's energy releases you from a state of nervous and anxiety into one of serenity and tranquility. Allow Fluorite to cleanse both your mind and immediate environment. The stone is known not just to clarify our mental forces but also our space. It is known to be one of the best absorbent crystals that neutralize negativity from our environment and infuse it with greater balance. The dazzling rainbow colors of Fluorite are known to cleanse a person spiritually while filling their space with happiness, contentment, and peace. You can either sleep or meditate with a Fluorite to develop greater mental clarity and balance between various chakras of our body.

Fluorite's healing properties or characteristics include enhanced clarity of mind and sharper focus. It can be used while studying, learning, or picking up a new skill. The stone can also be utilized for eliminating inflammation within our body, reducing cold symptoms, healing our mucous membrane. This is an all-powerful crystal that is known to possess several benefits and characteristics.

Hematite

Hematite is an iron-rich stone that is known for its intense grounding and connection with the earth. In ancient Greece, the hematite was known as the "bloodstone" owing to the rich red shade of iron prevalent in nature.

The crystal's metaphysical healing characteristics include an intensely grounding effect as the stone is closely linked with our Root Chakra. Its grounding energy reminds us of our existence and supports us where wealth and finances are concerned.

Hematite's iron content helps us cleanse our blood, enhance blood circulation, regulate irregular menstrual flow, and support our heart. The crystal can also be utilized for eliminating stress, nervousness, and anxiety while calming your nerves and the nervous system.

Kyanite

Kyanite is known as the stone of emotion. It assists our mind in forming pathways where there weren't any previously, more so in terms of creating a meditation practice and emotional development. Kyanite doesn't gather negative energy so it doesn't have to be cleaned. This is why it can also be used for cleansing other spaces and crystals. It is a soothing blue-green crystal that is often connected with the sky and is therefore known to be healing and supportive to our nerves.

Kyanite's metaphysical healing properties include enhancing a person's psychic abilities while deepening meditation and opening channels for spiritual development. It can also be utilized for assisting those who are passing through death and make the transition into the other world easier.

Kyanite also possesses a plethora of physical properties such as eliminating pain in the throat and enhanced communication. It is also utilized for reducing headaches, eye pain (staring at the computer for sustained periods), and brow tension.

Blue Topaz

Blue Topaz is the stone of creativity and inventiveness. It is symbolic of our mind and potential for creating. It can help activate the mind to master things quickly and retain facts/information that can be accessed for years. It is also amazing for stirring up creativity and opening our mind to innovative ideas.

Blue topaz's metaphysical properties include connecting with guiding angels, spirit guides, and loved ones who've passed away. Harness the power of blue topaz for expanding your mind, opening the doors of your soul, and aligning in the realm of spirits.

The stone also has munificent physical healing properties. It is known to help with mental ailments, eye diseases, eye sight issues, and resorting loss of taste.

Moonstone

Moonstone is known to be the stabilizer stone of the crystal world. It is connected with the feminine forces and moon, which makes it an ideal crystal for building harmony, strength, and intuition. Moonstone was believed to be the stones of ancient deities across cultures. It is seen as a sacred, powerful, and regal stone.

Moonstone's metaphysical properties include opening up to the universe and the other world. It is also effective for fighting materialism and regulating the ego.

Some physical healing properties of moonstone are aiding the pituitary gland and digestive system, controlling obesity, reducing water retention, regulating hormones, and eliminating menstrual problems.

Clear or Crystal Quartz

Crystal quartz is the spirit stone. It is one of the most widely recognized crystals in the world. It is viewed as a realm of light in the metaphysical universe.

Crystal quartz bestows a person with several metaphysical benefits since it holds the entire color spectrum. Quartz can be utilized for everything from fulfilling desires to prayers to manifestation from the spiritual and physical world. Meditate with crystal quartz while programming or infusing the crystal with intentions. Filling your quartz with the right intention can help increase its positive vibrations, and therefore, chances of being fulfilled. One can simply carry this crystal to increase their vibrations, while also increasing manifestation of dreams.

Clear Quartz is clearly the rockstar among crystals. It illuminates your spirit like no other stone and is believed to bring about a profound sense of clarity. Known to be a universal healer, Clear Quartz is linked to all our body's chakras to bring about a sense of harmony, serenity, and balance. It possesses the ability to be programmed for manifestation more effectively than any other crystal. Placing a clear quartz on your body or pocket/bag/wallet helps to manifest your deepest intentions like never before.

Clear quartz is the undisputed king of the quartz category. It is one of the most flourishing minerals found on earth. Clear Quartz can be developed in a variety of environments and can be found on almost every continent. It is precisely for this reason that it is associated with several cultures and civilizations across the world. Quartz literally means ice in Greek. The ancient Greek philosophers believed that the transparent Crystal Quartz was a permanent ice. They believed it was so cold that it would never thaw.

What is truly unique about Crystal Quartz is every culture had their meaning or interpretation of this miracle stone. For instance, in Japan, it was the ideal or flawless jewel since the Japanese believed the stone represented space and patience. On the other hand, the indigenous North Americans believed the stone to be a sentient being and fed it food and others offerings out of reverence. In South and Central America, the quartz symbolized a vessel that held spirits of ancestors. These crystals were therefore often carved in the form of a human skull and utilized as a talisman. Similarly in Scotland, spheres were carved out of the crystals. People believed that clear quartz possesses the metaphysical property to heal several illnesses among their cattle. In the present day, Crystal Quartz is known to possess multiple metaphysical attributes. It stands for clarity, concentration, and manifestation. If you want to manifest something in life, Crystal Quartz is one of the best stones to work with. Its clear energies bring about a sense of focus and clarity while helping you accomplish what you truly desire in life.

Quartz properties such as programmability are vital to manifesting intentions. For programming the quartz with our intentions, it is important to hold it in your palm and focus on exactly what you desire to transfer or infuse in the crystal. The Crystal Quartz is known to have a striking memory (which is why quartz is used in electronics for storing a large amount of data). The crystal's memory downloads our intentions and facilitates the manifestation of goals through our ability to amplify these intentions much like it happens in technological devices. Quartz healing properties increase any energy that surrounds it on is instilled into it. Cleanse your stone occasionally to ensure it retains its positive energy.

Quartz properties can help us connect with and help various chakras, awarding it the reputation of a big daddy healer. Clear Quartz is especially valuable when it comes to activating the energy of our crown chakra. This chakra dominates how we perceive various situations. Quartz allows us to open the mind and gain free from negative thoughts and perspective to arrive at a more positive and enlightened viewpoint. It has several metaphysical properties from growing our consciousness to encouraging open communication to stimulating our body's chakras. For people who need more mental clarity, clear quartz has plenty of healing properties that will not just eliminate energy blockages but also facilitate the free flow of energy throughout our body.

If you are using the Crystal Quartz to energize or cleanse your space from the Feng Shui perspective, it is best placed on a window sill. Its amplification properties will radiate positive energy attracted from the sun and moon into the entire room.

Looking to meditate with the crystal quartz? For practicing meditation with the crystal quartz, you can either infuse your intentions into a mantra or utilize a mantra for strengthening the meditation after transferring intentions into a crystal. There are several mantras that can be used with quartz. For example, "I am crystal clear about my goals, dreams, and intentions." Repeating this mantra while meditating can make you even more strong-willed and determined about your purpose. It also facilitates visualization of your objectives. Lie down and place the clear quartz on your third eye to develop greater clarity and easy flow into the crown chakra.

Not limited to metaphysical properties, quartz also has several physical healing energies such as stimulating the immune system, boosting the functioning of our body's circulatory systems, and boosting the flow of the body's qi energy.

Turquoise

Turquoise is the protection stone that has been much sought after by everyone from ancient kinds to shaman practitioner to wizards. Recognized as a symbol of knowledge, enlightenment, and wisdom, turquoise has been a part of almost every ancient culture as the crystal of protection.

Some of the metaphysical properties of turquoise include strengthening the body's meridians while supporting meditation and intuition. Owing to rich blue hue, it is also associated with our Throat Chakra, which represents clarity in communication. People carry turquoise with them as a protection talisman as well as to leverage the ancient knowledge and wisdom it transmits.

Some physical healing characteristics of turquoise include helping with ailments related to neck, throat, ears, and brain. Turquoise is deeply connected with our psychic realm, thus making it a wonderful stone when it comes to clearing blockages and supporting a healthy energy flow throughout the body.

Jade

Jade is the crystal family's dream stone. It is a dynamic crystal found in a variety of colors across the world. The color is determined by a particular region and was one of the most extensively utilized stones in olden times. It has been worshipped across civilizations and cultures for its innumerable metaphysical as well as physical healing characteristics. It is one of the most widely and consistently used stones known to mankind.

At a metaphysical level, Jade symbolizes nobility, ideals, and principles. This crystal is also linked with the heart to help us learn and accept the truth, demonstrate love while guiding us to experience shamanic realms in our dreams.

Jade is also known to possess several physical healing properties. With its connection to the heart, it is amazing for filtering toxins, cleansing our body in its entirety through blood purification. It can also be used for easing joint pain and speeding up the post-surgery healing process.

Amethyst

Amethyst is a common new age stone along with quartz and selenite. It can be widely found across several corners of the world. This stunning purple crystal is known to several benefits including manifestation.

Amethyst's metaphysical properties include connecting with our heart's desires and life's higher purpose and eventually manifesting them. This powerful crystal is closely linked with the body's upper chakras, assisting us in drawing the ethereal into our physical realm. This all-powerful, manifestation encompassing stone is also connected with living the life of our dreams.

Amethyst's physical healing properties include enhancing the function of our nervous system, balancing hormones, relief from headaches, alleviating neck tension, and dealing with insomnia. Keep the amethyst under your pillow before going to bed. You'll awaken feeling more rested and raring to go with your manifestation, goals, and dream life.

The stone is known to possess plentiful healing properties, including being a highly protective stone. Since it's closely linked with the crown chakra, amethyst is valuable when it comes to purifying our mind and cleansing it from any destructive thoughts. This also includes negativity related to anxiety, stress, and exhaustion. This is exactly why several people meditate with this big day stone to eliminate the darkness around them. Amethyst's healing properties are valuable when it comes to stress-related work since the stone is also linked with abundance. It relieves stress while radiating prosperity. Amethyst properties include promoting intuition, healing, and communication. They are also known to increase work effectiveness.

Despite the fact that it isn't a rare stone or is widely found across the world, amethyst is one of history's most revered stones. For many centuries, it has been seen as the go-to crystal for all things religious and spiritual. Found in several places throughout Bolivia, Africa, Europe, Russia, Mexico, Canada, and USA, the stone has a thriving history of splendid civilizations with its gorgeous, saturated beauty. While the Neolithic people of Europe used it a mere decorative prop during 25,000 B.C., the ancient Romans and Greeks utilized the power of amethyst in multiple ways. They crafted amulets and jewelry out of it. It was these civilizations that placed a high premium of amethyst as a stone. The operating belief was that amethyst was synonymous with elegance and luxury. As such, it was used in crowns and scepters. Christian bishops sported amethyst in rings. Amethyst's shade (purple) symbolized royalty and a spiritual/religious allegiance!

Members of the clergy sported amethyst on their crosses since its symbolized celibacy and purity. It was believed that the high priest of Israel's breastplate was also decorated with a stunning amethyst as one of its stones (the ninth one). It is believed that there were ten stone in all upon which the names of various Israeli tribes were engraved. Amethyst is believed to be one of these stones.

Amazonite

Amazonite is the stone of courage that calms one's spirit and heals the soul with its soothing green color. The stone empowers us the person who wears it to seek and express their inner truth with bravery, conviction, truth, courage, confidence, and boldness without getting increasingly emotional.

For people who feel their mind is polluted with destructive and toxic energy may find Amazonite highly cleansing and healing. Often, pain experienced in the past leads to energy blocks in our current life. This may manifest itself in several forms such as difficulty in expressing yourself or creative/productivity slumps. By enveloping your heart and throat chakras with more loving and nurturing energy, amazonite opens us to releasing the hurtful energy that was holding us back. This allows us to express ourselves more effectively in all aspects of life.

When it comes to healing crystals, people generally say that the crystal picks you instead of you picking the crystal. If the Amazonite has picked you, it is an indication that you need to be told the truth, even if it is hurtful. Amazonite's powerful properties are a reminder that you need to be heard. This is a strong throat chakra stone with healing properties that help us conquer fear and uncertainty. With Amazonite by your side, you do not have to fear confrontation and judgment. This wonder crystal facilitates our ability to express our true selves freely. There are multiple societal filters, including gender, culture, and other factors, which make our inner truth hazy. However, amazonite's powerful properties guide us in the right direction into a more authentic line of existence where truth and honesty prevail.

The best way to use amazonite is to meditate with it. This can be the ideal way to take stock of your body, mind, and spirit. Look at the stone serene contemplation. Allow it to dissolve or dissipate any negative thoughts that occur on the surface. Keep in mind that there is a strong reason Amazonite chose you. It is a conspicuous signal that the process of soothing and healing your emotional wounds have begun.

Besides being attractive and aesthetic, the Amazonite also offers us the wisdom to identify kindness by energizing and supporting our heart chakra. This mighty stone gently instills the spirit of trusting our truest intentions and freeing our soul from confusing influences that are attempting to throw us off the path. Life may appear confusing and overwhelming sometimes. However, Amazonite lends order to confusion with its ethereal light of hope, expression, and love.

The healing powers of Amazonite teach us to love and accept the truth along with our inner, authentic selves. Meditate with Amazonite crystal, while also channelize its infinite powers. At times, we have to lose ourselves to find ourselves.

Amazonite's metaphysical healing characteristics include balancing, soothing, and cleansing the body's chakras. It helps reduce emotional trauma housed in the body, prevents this trauma from growing into physical ailments. This powerful crystal is also beneficial for harmonizing and balancing the connection between logical reasoning and intuition for a positive balance that keeps us wise and grounded.

Amazonite's physical properties typically include general health and well-being. It is known to be beneficial for our entire body. Utilize the crystal for soothing rashes, clearing skin acne, and preventing wound based infection.

Rose Quartz

Rose Quartz is widely known to be the love or romance stone. It is closely connected with the heart and expressing unconditional love to one's self as well as other people. This beautiful pink quartz is associated with finding love and enhancing already existing relationships.

Some metaphysical properties of rose quartz include inviting love into one's life, assisting in giving love, and attracting one's soul mate. Rose quartz is related to all things heart. Wear this crystal or carry it to open yourself to finding the ideal partner or true love if you are single. If you are in a relationship, rose quartz can strengthen and nurture your existing bond with your partner. This is the crystal to wear if you are looking for love in a new or existing relationship.

The physical healing properties of rose quartz include emotional healing, release from negative emotions that are holding you back from attracting true love into your life, enhancing blood circulation, and reducing blood pressure. Rose quartz is also effective for stabilizing palpitations or skipped heartbeats along with releasing tension and stress.

Garnet

Garnet is the stone of health, wellness, and creativity, and is found in a range of hues and compositions. It is known for its characteristics of facilitating health, creativity, and a grounding spirit.

Some metaphysical healing properties of garnet include eliminating inhibitions and taboos and fostering creative thinking. It brings clarity of thought, wisdom, and free thinking. Garnet's vibrations allow the spirit to be part of the physical realm while opening creativity and communication channels with one's inner self to facilitate outward expression.

The physical properties of garnet are stimulating metabolism, getting the body to move, fighting blood clotting and bleeding, and enhancing the sexual libido and increasing sexual desire.

Opal

Opal is the eye stone, which is a spectrum of bright, eclectic colors when seen under light. It is connected with the Third Eye chakra or psychic powers (intuition). Opal's energies trigger happiness, positivity, optimism, appreciation, and a broad sense of happiness and well-being. There are more than ten distinct kinds of opal crystals, all of which originate from various regions of the world with different characteristics. The crystal has several metaphysical and physical properties that can be harnessed to live a physically, psychologically, and spiritually fulfilling life.

Opal's metaphysical properties include turning into a prism for our aura and drawing light spectrum into our spiritual and energy realm. It can increase vibrant energy within the soul, which isn't common to other crystals. Utilize opal for awakening psychic, intuitive, and mystical properties as a means for helping us connect with our spiritual realms.

Similarly, opal's physical healing characteristics include supporting our eye health and enhancing vision. It is also used for stimulating learning, retention of information, and regulating neurotransmitter disturbances.

Lapis Lazuli

Lapis lazuli is the dazzling blue stone of truth. It is a vibrant, olden, and much sought after stone. It has often been connected with luxury, elegance, and royalty while possessing celestial properties that guide those within the physical realm with intelligence, wisdom, and judgment.

Some healing metaphysical properties of lapis lazuli include activating ethereal upper chakras and empowering our Throat Chakra for clarity of communication and expressing oneself effortlessly. This mysterious and intriguing crystal facilitates inner observation, clarity, and truth as it helps in the exploration of our spiritual realm.

Some physical healing properties of lapis lazuli include facilitating healing of the throat and vocal cords. Owing to strong associations with the brain, the crystal is also believed to help those suffering from ADD or Attention Deficit Disorder by helping our mind focus on releasing unwanted and negative thoughts.

Carnelian

Carnelian infuses life into a party. It stands for creativity, confidence, and energy. The sheer energy of carnelian is motivating and offers a vibrancy rush in the sacral chakra for triggering our inner star. Tap into the carnelian's exciting and energetic properties to offer it a sense of power that proves beneficial for those looking to transcend creative blocks for embarking on new assignments, projects, jobs, and businesses. With a carnelian close to you, you can be assured of impressing other people with your radiance, strength, and charm.

Referred to as the singer's stone, the Carnelian crystal is known to be a dazzling, warm, and confidence radiating stone that possesses the power of expression. It is known as the stone of choice of most performers. Created out of extensively available microcrystalline quartz, the vibrant and peppy chalcedony version derives its features (specks, bands, and stripes) from iron impurities that look awesome when polished.

In ancient Egyptian civilization, polished Carnelian crystal was a much sought after stone in combination with Onyx and Lapis Lazuli. It was utilized in necklaces and collars made for the royals. The Romans were also known to utilize a huge number of Carnelian crystals embedded in gold for finger rings. Owing to its hardness, the carnelian crystal was also embedded into cameo rings that represented personal emblems of figurines of ancient gods, a highly popular fashion in second century CE.

That Carnelian is known for its healing properties is no secret. During the middle ages, healers held Carnelian crystal's healing properties in high regard. It was viewed as a mechanism for easing stress, anxiety, and tension. Featured in multiple hues varying from brown to orange to red, the stone is known to eliminate worry and bring about a sense of playfulness and spontaneity with its dazzling, warm vibes.

Besides being stunningly beautiful, the Carnelian crystal is symbolic of the warm cauldron of the body's three lower chakras. It is often closely linked with taking courageous action with warm and fiery properties that stimulate our root chakra. Thus Carnelian helps in the circulation of vital energy to our center that holds our deepest sexual fantasies/desires and creative instincts. Since the stone is closely associated with performance, whether sexual performance or on the stage, the properties of Carnelian can make you the star! Its healing features make it's a fiery performance oriented companion that offers performers the ability to overcome their fears and anxiety. Place a Carnelian beside you as a piece of jewelry or stone (in your pocket, wallet, or purse) to swing into action with the right doses of self-assuredness and confidence.

Whether you are preparing for an upcoming job interview, business negotiation, or audition, carrying a Carnelian with you can help you rock the opportunity even under extreme stress. Highly popular among performers/actors, Carnelian draws out our hidden talent by creating a sense of balance between our creativity and focus, between the left and right brain regions.

Are you in the mood for some love and romance? Carnelian crystal is closely associated with Rose Quartz that helps bring about a sense of harmony between the vibration of love and sexual energy. When the two stones are kept on the heart chakra, it helps us establish a connection with our sexual and romantic side. To make the most of its grounding effects, utilize a healing layout that includes stones placed on your lower abdomen to energize and cleanse your root chakra, the energy center anchoring us to the earth's inherent forces.

The Carnelian crystal not just increases valor and confidence, but also purifies our blood and enhances circulation at a cellular level, which is a must-do during highly stressful and anxiety-laden situations. For actors and other entertainers, a perpetual flow of support, positivity, and warmth when all eyes are on them is crucial for their performance. When you need to demonstrate your best side, put a Carnelian in your bath while infusing the water with its powerful healing properties. This can be a highly effective treatment just before hitting a large performance oriented event. Allow your fear, anxiety, worry, and stress to melt away. Keep repeating this affirmation, "I am bold, confident, and dazzling."

Perform a Carnelian meditation to explore your true passion. If you are confused about where your true passion lays or the path you need to embark upon, meditate with a Carnelian. Find a comfortable spot to meditate and witness the sunset. This represents the end of the day and the start of a new one. This is the ideal time to hold the pause button. Enjoy and soak up the moment completely while holding the Carnelian on your second chakra, just under the navel. You may experience a sudden inspiration jolt or the creativity brain bulb of your brain may switch on. Close your eyes and sit in contemplation to question yourself about what brings you excitement, happiness, and joy in life at this point of time. Pay attention to the first thoughts that occur to you. Meditate on the steps that are to be taken to reach there. Your ally, the Carnelian will help you concentrate your energy on what really matters filtering out the negative and unwanted.

Chapter Seven: Intention Setting With Crystals

What is Intention?

You've heard crystals are powerful when it comes to setting intentions. However, what are these intentions? And how can you harness the power of crystals to set intentions and manifest your dream life? Here's decoding intentions for you.

Honestly, if you don't know where you are heading or what you hope to accomplish with the crystals, they won't do much for you. Intention setting is integral to the process of making crystals work for you. If you don't know where you are heading, how will you reach there? If you have the fire in your belly to enrich your physical, mental, spiritual, and professional development, you'll know what exactly you want. If you have a compelling desire to make your dreams come true, you'll set powerful intentions. Remember, your life is nothing but an expression of your most dominant thought vibrations. What you think is what you become.

Intention, as defined by TheFreeDictionary.com, is "a course of action that one intends to follow, an aim that guides action, and objective." Similarly, Merriam-Webster defines it as "a determination to act in a certain way." An intention is a positive and precise statement about an outcome you desire to experience. Intentions can also be termed goals, visions, and dreams that guide or determine our behavior, actions, attitudes, thoughts, and choices. Our intentions set in motion become real experiences.

One can set an intention for a single in their life – physical, spiritual, or emotional. Intentions almost always begin with clear mental visuals of the final goal. They require focus, actions, and positive energy to manifest into reality. This is where your crystals come into the picture. Crystals can lend your intentions powerful positive energy and keep you focused on your mental visuals or goals. This is especially true when you meditate with crystals or use them during the process of visualizing your goals.

Intentions offer a clear framework to help us set priorities, utilize our time judiciously, and align ourselves with resources needed to manifest our goals. The entire process of setting goals and working towards these intentions is a declaration to yourself and the universe that you are dead serious about accomplishing your goals and visions. A powerful, energized, precise, and positive intention repels everything that is not aligned with it. Similarly, a weak intention attracts distractions. A powerful and energized intention attracts the core of what it stands for.

Crystals are powerful objects when it comes to intention setting because they hold massive energy of the natural forces or universe. It can be used as an anchor to exchange energies and communicate with the universe. When you set an intention with a crystal in your hand, you are declaring your desires to the universe and experiencing a surge of positive energy while doing so. This positive energy in turn is capable of guiding and propelling your actions in the right direction by constantly reminding you of your goals. Every time you look at the crystal, you will be reminded of your intentions because it holds the energy or vibrations of your thoughts.

Intention setting is an effective and powerful exercise when it comes to manifesting everything from happiness to wealth to good health and stability. From what we feed ourselves to the career journey we embark upon, everything originates from intention. Intention setting is the first step when it comes to manifesting our dreams or living our true destiny. Without a clear intention, you are like a driver with the best map and vehicle in the world without knowing where to go. There is no destination even if you have the best tools to reach your destination. When it comes to activating the power of crystals, leveraging the Law of Attraction, and following pretty much any other manifestation ritual, intention is the first step of the process.

The Basics of Intention Setting

Setting intentions is a wonderful and powerful tool for helping us accomplish what we truly seek in life. They facilitate our happiness, peace, and fulfillment. Intentions offer us insights into our deepest values, purpose, and aspirations. They allow us to exist in the present while aiming for new accomplishments and glory. While our objectives are the outcome we desire, setting intentions is a tiny step that lets us experience a sense of accomplishment even if the goal is not met.

When we set intentions and state those intentions aloud, it aligns the energies of our mind and heart to build a meaningful purpose. Whether you choose an intention for each day, week, or year, it helps you stay centered, aligned, and focused in the midst of chaos. Begin every morning by infusing your intention with energy from healing stones that are ideal for complementing a meditation practice. This ensures that you create energy and space for manifesting these intentions.

Combine this practice with daily mantra recitation or say your affirmations. Repeating this mantra all the time will allow your subconscious mind to absorb its energies and act in alignment with what you keep saying. A daily mantra or affirmation can keep us stay firmly focused on our objectives as we go about our daily routine.

Setting powerful intentions begins with goals that are in alignment with our values, purpose, objectives, and aspirations. Intentions don't hold much weight unless they are empowered with a strong reason for why you desire to accomplish something. Ensure you write your thoughts in a free flowing manner while setting and creating powerful intentions that add more value to your life.

Begin by deciding what truly matters to you in life. Your values and beliefs power your actions. Recognizing what your core values are will help you set intentions that when fulfilled lead to happiness and contentment. If you haven't done it already, write down five things that are most important in your life or matter the most. For instance, spiritual development, happiness, compassion, health, knowledge, wealth, and so on.

Explore several aspects of your life that need to be upgraded. Goals should hold more than a single aspect of our life. Make your intentions all-encompassing, though you should focus on accomplishing one goal at a time. This is to ascertain that your personal development accomplishes its fullest potential. Consider enhancing your relationships, professional life, social life, health, community contribution, and spirituality. Use your inherent values for guiding your actions and thinking about the goals you intend to set in different areas of your life.

Be specific, purposeful, and thoughtful. When we are setting intentions for our goals, they should be specific and laser-focused on what we desire to accomplish. Determine by when you wish you achieve a goal and why you want to chase it. Think about everything you need to do to achieve the goal, in addition to anticipating potential roadblocks along the way.

Rather than setting multiple intentions and goals at a time to lead your mind into a state of chaos, focus on a single goal each month. Set positive intentions that will help you accomplish these goals. For example, if your objective is to deepen your spiritual practices, you can set an intention of "existing in the present moment" during meditation. This allows you to free your mind from things that have happened in the past and are likely to happen in the future. Keep your daily and weekly intentions simply to feel centered and bring about change. If you experience success with an intention, after a while, try setting another intention with a similar goal. In the above example, it can be something like, "not reacting impulsively or emotionally to everything that happens to me" or "keeping my emotions and angry reactions in check." Your goal in both these intentions is the same – spiritual development. However, in the former, you are focusing on living in the present, while in the later, it is about managing your emotions.

While setting intentions, use healing stones and crystal energy jewelry to enhance the intention setting process. Wearing a crystal whose energy is aligned with your intentions acts as a content reminder for our intention. Think about this – you wear an energy crystal bracelet in your hand while meditating, practicing visualization, or setting intentions. Each time you look at the bracelet, you will be reminded of your goals, desires, and intentions. Place a crystal on your intentions after you finished writing them. Every time you view the crystals, they will bring your intention alive and guide you to act in the right direction. You are literally living with your intention. Intentions are intangible goals or thoughts that have certain energies or vibrations. These energies and vibrations assume a tangible form when you set intentions with the help of crystals. The crystals become your intention energy. Healing crystals also help amplify the energy of our goals and intentions by placing them out there into the universe to manifest them quicker.

One of the most important things to keep in mind during intention setting is that intentions help create our present moment. Irrespective of whether you've accomplished your goals, intentions align you with the primary reason you desire to accomplish these goals. Intentions help set and create more value in our everyday life by offering motivation to accomplish something in the present instead of future. Our success is dependent on doing one thing a day to support the intention we set.

Why intention? Because it sets into motion the potent energy of your thoughts. Your purpose is launched into motion whether you are aware of it or not. With their unique and powerful vibrations, crystals can facilitate the process of intention setting. Pretty much like written lists, vision board, or written affirmations (or positive statements about what we intend to become or create written as if they are already our present reality), crystals become the anchors or visual reminders of our intentions. Remember, how we come to associate our goals and certain visuals with these crystals if we use them during the process of visualization or meditation? This is why crystals are awesome when it comes to incorporating them into a meditation, visualization, or intention setting routine. Here is a four-step intention setting process to set crystal clear goals or intentions.

Pick your stone

Every crystal is linked with a clear meaning, energy, feeling, and intention. You will feel it intuitively when you begin connecting with your crystals at a deeper level. It may not happen immediately and you absolutely mustn't force yourself to connect with your crystals at any point in time. If it doesn't happen immediately, it will happen over a period of time when you cleanse, activate, and nurture your crystals.

How do you buy your favorite outfit or pair of shoes? Besides the prices, how do you decide that you want to pick up one item over the other? We are obviously drawn to some pieces more than the others. This is true for crystals too, only here, you are drawn to them on a deeper level. We are pulled towards some crystals over others due to their color, feel, smell, properties, patterns, and more. The most important factor that we don't realize at the outset is that we are subconsciously drawn to stones that reflect or hold the energy we are trying to attract into our life.

For example, you may be trying to attract unconditional love or a soul mate in your life, and therefore feel naturally drawn to the crystal of love or romance, the rose quartz. We are not just randomly drawn to crystals. You may feel like you are instinctively drawn to a stone. However, that instinct is nothing more than your subconscious mind communicating with the stone to help attract what it is attempting to draw into your life. At a deeper level, we are all yearning to bring one thing or another into our life. The crystals we are attracted towards is our subconscious thought energy that is drawn to a stone that radiates the energy of what we want more of in our life.

While picking a stone, focus on its shape, pattern, and color. Do not concentrate on the particular healing powers initially. Our intuition guides us in the direction of the stone that will best help us what we truly desire in life.

Cleanse

Once you choose a crystal, it is vital to cleanse it to eliminate any negative energies that it may absorb along the process of its creation. Other people may have handled the crystal before you, and it is highly likely that their energies have been passed on to the stone. Hence, clear your crystal from any unwanted or negative vibrations before you begin setting intentions. There are several elements and methods for cleansing or charging your crystals (refer the chapter on crystal cleansing).

Set Intention

Hold the crystal in your hand (preferably the dominant one) and clear your mind from any unwanted, unnecessary, and negative thoughts. This may take a while. It doesn't happen in a flash so give your self more time. Don't push thoughts out of your mind or force yourself to clear the mind. If you are setting an intention for the first time, be patient with yourself. It'll come with time and practice. When picking an intention, always think of the bigger picture. For example, "I want to make two million dollars" doesn't focus on the larger picture. Instead set an intention such as, "I wish to attract new money making opportunities in my life, along with the ability and courage to make the most of these opportunities." This focuses on the larger picture and sounds like a more practical and doable intention. It throws more clarity on how you would like to go about fulfilling the intention.

Calm your mind and start focusing on your crystals. Infuse them with the intention you have picked for them. Be clear about your intention while focusing on the bigger picture. Describe your intention loudly. Say a few positive affirmations related to your intention. Repeat the words until the energy connects with your crystal and your subconscious mind absorbs what you want to manifest. It is important for the energy of your intention to connect with the crystal. How will you know the intention is set? Your intuition will guide you, pretty much like everything else related to crystals.

Revisiting the intention

Place the crystal on your desk, under the pillow, or adjacent to your bed to ensure it serves as a reminder for your positive goals and intentions. When we use crystals while setting intentions, they become the physical carriers of this intention setting energy. We can revisit our positive intentions simply by looking at these crystals from time to time. Keep revisiting and resetting your intentions every week to stay on the path of your journey. Stay conscious and mindful of the energy you are attracting. Being positive will help you attract even more positive energy to help manifest your desires.

Meditating with Crystals

Several people have observed through individual experiences that holding a crystal or being near one has positively impacted their consciousness. This effect can be positively channelized by picking the right crystals and positioning them effectively. Again, though this phenomenon has not been studied or researched scientifically, practitioners have experienced it and described it in detail.

How does this happen? It isn't really clear why or how this happens but there may be a reasonable explanation for it. The lattice structure of crystals may be responsible for this. By their inherent definition, crystals display a repetitive, symmetrical lattice pattern, much like a three-dimensional grid. Different crystals come with different patterns, structures, and colors. It is often believed that our aura is activated, focused, and cleansed by the presence of a crystal in our energy field. The aura stretches several feet across our body, which is why the being in close range of a crystal is enough for boosting focus, enhancing our mood, and meditating more effectively.

The best part about meditation is that though it's remarkably powerful, healing and fulfilling, it doesn't need anything other than our mind and body. However, using specific elements can help strengthen our meditation practice owing to the positive and powerful vibrations they carry. These elements enhance your meditation while lifting your state of consciousness. This is exactly why crystals are effective when it comes to complementing a disciplined and consistent meditation practice.

Don't be too rattled by how and why they work. Instead, focus on making the most of these crystals by harnessing their positive attributes. Crystals can either be instinctively picked according to certain noticeable patterns. Try holding a crystal in your dominant hand while trying to empty your mind and attract an inflow of positive thoughts. Observe your feelings closely. How does a particular crystal make you feel? If it makes you feel peaceful, positive and empowered, it may just be what you are looking for.

Using crystals is a wonderful way to enhance your meditation practice, visualization, and intention setting (pro tip – combine all three for best results). Clear quartz is ideal for developing greater mental clarity, while colored stones or crystals can be good for chakra stimulation and clearing. A crystal can also be held in your hand to increase focus during regular meditation or if you wish to meditate upon the crystal itself. Crystal meditation is primarily used in cleansing and opening the body's chakras by using the right correct crystal on the same colored chakra and then attempting to breathe through the chakra. Certain crystals are closely associated with each of our body's seven chakras or energy centers. Their vibrations match the energy of these chakras and hence these stones are powerful when it comes to chakra healing.

Choose a crystal you feel a natural affinity for. Don't go for big stones in the beginning. Buy smaller and easier to hold crystals that cost a few dollars instead of splurging big on putting together a beneficial collection. Once you notice the positive effects of certain crystals, you can decide to invest more in them.

Before meditating, ensure that you create a relaxed, comfortable, and calm situation where you have sufficient time to meditate. Pick a space that is positive, distraction-free, and spiritually charged (burn incense or candles). Avoid meditating when you are in a distracted frame of mind or do not have too much time at hand. Turn off all gadgets, pull up the curtains, lock your door, and plug in your earphones.

Use a more universal or all-compassing stone like amethyst while meditating. However, that shouldn't stop you from using any other healing crystal you are drawn to or feel a sense of connection with. Amethyst is a purple quartz that is known to be an awesome meditation stone. Its name literally means it can counter the effects of alcohol (methanol –alcohol). It is known to be one of the most spiritually infused stones and is associated with our Third Eye chakra or intuition. Since this is a more spiritual and psychic energy stone, it makes for an effective meditation companion. Amethyst can facilitate better mental clarity, development of wisdom and insights, and a feeling of fulfillment.

Hold the crystal in your hands while setting an intention. Allow yourself to experience the magnetism and powerful energy properties of the stone. Let its energy permeate your entire space and energy field. Visualize your intentions specifically in the mind's eye. What do you desire? What do you want to accomplish? Imagine everything in detail. This makes the work of your crystals easier. It offers them a clear direction and sense of clarity, which makes your meditation practice even more effective. Don't let this creep you out, but your crystals are actually hearing you. They are forces of the earth that hold energies which are capable of communicating with you at the psychic and subconscious level. When you are able to establish a clear intention, you talk to them more effectively and thus help them assist you in your endeavors, goals, or intentions. Makes sense? Crystals help you accomplish a higher purpose when you clarify when you speak clearly to them.

Close your eyes. Sit in a relaxed position or the floor or a chair. Allow yourself to slip into a peaceful, relaxed, and undisturbed mental state. There is no past or future. You are here and now in the present. Focus on the present. Concentrate on the ebb and flow of your breath. Avoid forcing yourself to breathe in a particular manner. Simply go with the natural rhythm of your breath. Begin scanning your body mentally. Observe areas that have accumulated stress, tension, and pain. Make a conscious effort to relax these areas and eliminate tension from them.

Think of this as an energy flow between you and your crystal pretty much like you are conversing at a deeper level. You and the stone are both feeding on each other's energies and there is a palpable energy exchange happening between the two. Depending on your purpose or intention in a particular meditation session, focus on your energy source. For instance, if you desire to heal pain in a specific part of your body, concentrate on the exact pain area. Allow the powerful crystal vibrations to drift into that particular region.

There is no time limit for meditating with your crystals. Meditate for as long as you feel comfortable and connected with your crystals. Remember that though crystals are not integral to the practice of meditation, they can facilitate and enhance it. Crystals can act as valuable guides to set you along the path of your intention with peace, power, and positivity.

Once you've completed your meditation, gradually bring gentle movements into your hands and feet while opening your eyes. Ensure you store the crystals in a safe and positively infused space once you've finished using them so that they are always available to guide you whenever you need healing and energizing.

Chapter Eight: Simple and Effective Ways to Use Crystals

Once you pick your crystals, what is the next step? One of the most vital yet overlooked aspects of using crystals is intention setting. People often believe the energy of crystals often help them overcome certain challenging situations and problems in their life. However, the benefit that is most overlooked is using crystals for setting intentions or programming the mind. You can use it as a powerful medium for anchoring your thoughts, feelings, and intentions to keep visiting these over and over again. In simple words, it is your job to give your crystal a clear purpose. Think of them as allies that want to shower their powerful properties on you. However, you have to tell them what you want from them. They are communicating and vibrating energies that are capable of interacting with your own thought energies. Once you explicitly state your intention or let the crystal know its purpose, it is easier for you to connect with your crystal. As a beginner, you may struggle to establish a connection with your crystals. However, don't be freaked out if you don't experience an instant connection with these energy objects. It will come over a period of time. Patience is the key when it comes to connecting with crystals. It takes time for the energy exchange to take place. You may not feel the vibrations immediately.

When we are vibrating on a low energy frequency, our intentions fly out of the door faster than we can say quartz. This is when crystals can help you reconnect with your energy. By connecting with your programmed crystal, you are in effect connecting with your own limitless energy and potential. The programmed crystal serves as a reminder of our intention.

How does one program the crystal? Programming a crystal is easy. The first step of the crystal programming process is cleansing your crystal thoroughly to ward off negative and unwanted energies. You can use any of the cleansing methods described in this book depending on what resonates with you. It can be placed above a clear quartz crystal or selenite to cleanse it. Alternatively, you can bury the stone within the earth and allow our planet to infuse it with natural energy and goodness. Similarly, the crystal can be immersed in the smoke of a lighted sage stick. Another method is giving your crystal a moon bath on a full moon night by placing it on a windowsill and allowing the moon to cast its light on the stone for 4-5 hours.

Place the crystal in your hand and slowly close your eyes. Take a couple of deep breaths. Reflect upon your faith, Mother Nature, and everything that makes you happy. Reflect upon the purpose of your life and what you truly want to accomplish. This helps us connect with our highest energy vibrations. Our highest energy is often associated with a spiritual, philosophical, or religious belief.

If you are just getting started with using crystals, here are some simple yet powerful intention crystals for peace of mind, positivity, harmony, and balance. Not just are these crystals glittering beauties but they also possess plenty of healing properties that connect us to the earth and its abundance. They establish our connection with the forces that we originate from.

Clear Quartz – How to use it

Crystal quartz is one of the most popular crystals for beginners. It amplifies one's intentions, which makes it an important inclusion in your crystal collection. Clear quartz is also known to be the most versatile and multipurpose stone since it magnifies the energy of crystals that are around it. In effect, wands made of crystal quartz are generally used for reenergizing and cleansing other stones. This is owing to the belief that it possesses powerful cleansing benefits that are capable of counteracting energy blockages. Clear quartz can be used for a variety of purposes.

How to use your clear quartz crystal? Simply sit calmly with the stone in a space infused with positive energy and natural light. Go over your intention with the healing crystal in your hand while having complete faith in the power of its vibrations. This is the Earth's energy you are holding and harnessing.

Selenite - How to use it

Selenite is another powerful cleansing stone since it facilitates a positive vibration flow between you and several other crystals in your collection, which makes it one of the best crystals for beginners.

This versatile and all-purpose crystal quickly eliminates negative energy from our body and clears the aura around us. To cleanse the aura around you or within your energy field, simply move the selenite from your head to feet. Repeat this ritual multiple times until you feel completely at ease and refreshed with positive vibrations. Later, you'll experience a more restored sense of positivity, balance, protection, and harmony of a white light that connects you with powerful forces of the universe. You'll experience a release of negative energies and protection from the universe's all-powerful white light.

Shungite - How to use it

Shungite is one of the rarest crystals found on earth and contains antioxidants that lend it its powerful healing properties such as protection from harmful energies, especially energies that pose a hazard to our body. The rare crystal is also utilized for soothing anxiety and quickening the process of detoxification in our body. This is fundamentally a body cleansing and charging stone that infuses positive energy within our physical body. Since this healing crystal has potent effects on our body, it is ideal to introduce it gradually. Don't start using intensely right in the beginning or you'll end up being overwhelmed by its effects. The stone needs to be introduced gradually and steadily to harness its benefits to the fullest.

How best to use the powerful shungite? Place a shungite piece adjacent to your wi-fi hub, phone, computer, or any other electronic gadget. It will reduce the harmful effects of EMFs.

Amethyst – How to use it

Known for its strong spiritual and healing properties, amethyst is the perfect stone to cleanse and charge the energy of spaces. This means, you will be able to harness its benefits to the fullest when you place it in your home as a decorative item. This visually stunning rock also makes for a wonderful meditation companion since it facilitates all-round physical, mental, and spiritual development. Amethyst is known to increase our inner strength and offer spiritual protection.

While focusing on any intention, place amethyst in your bedroom or workplace to attract its calming and positive vibrations and abundance. This powerful crystal also works wonders when it comes to complementing a yoga, mindfulness, and meditation practice.

Citrine – How to use it

Citrine is another powerful crystal that is associated with the sun's energy. Its yellow, dazzling color reflects the all-powerful solar force and light. Since citrine is bestowed with the sun's natural energy, placing it on a windowsill may help harness its powers to the fullest. Allow its light energy and radiance to enter your space. Each day, citrine's natural light infusions restore and regenerate its strong vibrations. Believed to be one of the most powerful manifestation crystals, citrine is a must have in any beginner collection since it is known to be capable of transforming intentions into reality. Hold a citrine in your hand while meditating, setting intentions, or practicing visualizations. Citrines can be effective for virtually any manifestation ritual owing its powerful vibrations. It is especially potent when it comes to manifesting wealth, prosperity, power, and abundance.

If you have goals, dreams, or manifestation list, place a citrine on it to help transform these manifestations into reality quickly.

It doesn't necessarily have to be associated with faith or religion. It can also be some of a scientific connection. The most important point is to feel connected with faith or discipline. You determine what to term this energy. While you are in this region of light, energy, and love, ask your crystal to stay clear from unwanted and negative energy or earlier programming.

Say aloud in your head that "I ask that the highest love and light vibration connect with my highest self to clear all negative energy and any earlier programming. I command my crystal to hold the intention of.....Complete the sentence by adding three intentions for the crystal. These intentions are energies that you desire to hold. End the ritual by saying thank you thrice.

By saying it thrice, you are emphasizing that what you are intending to accomplish or asking for already exists in the universe. This is one of the biggest rules of manifestation. You believe what you are asking or intending to manifest is always yours. You don't perceive it as something you desire to get in a future date. This is where you operate from the "lack of" or "scarce" point of view, which creates a greater scarcity. When you want to manifest anything in life, think like it already exists in abundance within your life. This will attract more of it.

How Can I Work with Crystals?

Though the process of crystal healing can seem slightly complex and confounding to a beginner, it is simple to work with once you get accustomed to working with their energy. The key factor in every process of ritual involving healing crystals is your own energy. Working with crystals can be viewed as a form of spell casting. We've all seen a USB flash drive, right? These are little devices that are capable of storing and transferring information. Crystals perform the same function. Over the last few years, researchers have developed a small disk, which goes with the moniker of Superman memory crystal, which contains files that are written in fused quartz. Each of these files has the capacity to store 360 terabytes of data for a maximum of 14 billion years. Similarly, crystals can also be programmed to absorb, receive, transfer, and store feelings and emotions. Crystals can be attuned for a variety of purposes, including promoting health, wisdom, love, spiritual development, and prosperity. These are highly popular tools for manifestation in these areas. Your crystals are just short of talking to you. They are capable of everything from transferring energy to facilitating personal development.

Choosing a crystal can be one of the most overwhelming processes of working with crystals. Many beginners seek information about picking the right crystal as they're petrified of attracting any unwanted vibrations. Plus these crystals come within varying price ranges. If you plan to source your crystal from a brick and mortar store, intuition will be your favorite companion. Walk over to the crystal area, shut your eyes and run your hands over these crystals. Don't be embarrassed. Most shopkeepers who retail occult stuff have seen all this and more.

Now consider your magical intention. What would you like to accomplish with your crystals? Focus only on your manifestations. Place different crystals and gems on your hand. Observe your emotional and physiological sensations. Does your palm feel slightly warmer? Do you feel more energized? Does your entire being or spirit feel more serene? Keep in mind that there is no hierarchy of divinity when it comes to crystals or natural stones. Pick minerals that stirs your soul and makes you feel a sense of unison with the universe.

Another thing to keep in mind while selecting your crystals is to select the ones that are more universal or all-encompassing in their properties and application, especially if you are a beginner. When you gain a better understanding of stones, it's easy to pick stones that possess specific properties. It boils down to what you want the stone to do for you. Your intentions should match the crystal you pick.

If you are purchasing your crystal online, explore its intrinsic properties. Match the inherent functions of a crystal with your manifestation. For instance, if you are looking to manifest more abundance and prosperity, a citrine is ideal. Similarly, amethyst can be good for charging and cleansing a space. There are several choices for those beginning their crystal journey. When you are just starting, pick a more versatile and all-encompassing stone. Go for a time tested stone that is known to have multiple benefits. Also, avoid picking up too many stones at a time. Instead, go with a single crystal at a time to observe its effects. If you find it manifesting positive results, opt for stones with similar characteristics and properties. The thing about crystals is it doesn't have a single purpose. A crystal often performs more than one function or impacts different areas of our life. This makes them great tools to work with.

I've often been asked if crystals work? The simple answer is they work if you believe they do, pretty much like everything else in life. You have to have faith in your crystals. You have to believe that they contain the energy to transform your intentions into reality. Faith is what transforms a mere stone into an object of value.

Are you looking for an energy boost, grounding, manifestation, or any other benefit? Whatever your intention, there is a healing crystal that matches your requirements. Here are the most widely found healing properties in crystals. Understand that no crystal has a single purpose. Every crystal has multiple healing properties. However, certain stones are known to be especially valuable in specific areas. You can consider these as stones as healing stones. Here they are:

- o Chakra Balancing Crystals
- o Energizing Crystals
- o Grounding Crystals
- o Manifesting Crystals
- o Meditation Crystals
- o Record Keepers
- o Energy Shields
- o Love Crystals
- o Seeker Crystals
- o Soul Healing Crystals
- o Goddess Energy Crystals

Chapter Nine: Using Crystals with the 7 Laws of Attractions

The 7 Laws of Attraction are gaining attention all over the world for their effectiveness in manifesting goals and intentions. If you are wondering what these 7 laws of attraction are and how crystals can be used to amplify the effect of these 7 laws, read on.

What are the 7 Laws of Attractions?

1. Burning desire
2. Conceptualization and imagination
3. Affirmation
4. Confidence and focus
5. Profound Belief
6. Gratitude
7. Manifestation

1. Burning desire – Feel a burning desire for what you wish to manifest. Feeling a deep desire for what you wish to accomplish is the first and most vital step. Before you can get anything into the realm of reality, you must truly want it. And want it really bad. This feeling needs to be powerful, strong, and emotionally driven. The feelings and emotional frequencies must be strong for the manifestation process to be set into motion effectively. Use a crystal while visualizing your desires or setting an intention to pass on the powerful energy of your feelings into the stone. It will serve as a reminder of your goals. Each time you find your intention energy lowering, hold your crystal and look at it for a while.

2. **Conceptualization and imagination** – If you've seen *The Secret,* you will recall the part where the man sits in his chair to enthusiastically visualize his new car. He had an unshakable belief in his intention of sitting inside his dream car. Use the power of imagination and visualization to live your goals in your mind's eye before you experience them in real. This conditions your subconscious mind to focus on them and align your actions in line with goals. As a person forms a mental image of what he/she desires in their mind, they are in effect using their imagination to create reality. You must be able to view things in your imagination. They must be completely formed in your mind's vision before they are manifested. This is the exact process of creating visuals in your mind before desiring to manifest them.

Make your images or visuals as detailed and precise as possible. This gives your subconscious mind clear signals to work with. Imagine your visuals to be the map that guides your subconscious mind to guide you in the right direction. Make sense? When you feed precise ideas to your subconscious mind, it is capable of leading your actions in a clear direction to activate your mental forces for manifestation. Holding a crystal in your hand while visualizing and imagining your goals is a great way to increase your positive thought energy.

3. **Affirmation** – Affirmations are another potent force within the Law of Attraction realm to manifest what you desire. Talking about what you desire as if it is already yours using positive statements in the present tense is a great way to activate your subconscious and the universe into manifesting it. You must say these statements as if you believe it is to be and what you desire is truly yours. Do this on a daily basis to magnify its potential. Remember to use positive words and phrases. Do not focus on what you don't want. The universe or our subconscious mind doesn't understand negative

statements. It doesn't comprehend that you don't want something and will only end up giving you more of it if you focus on it. For instance, if you keep saying you don't want to be poor. The negative "don't" is eliminated from your affirmations. All the universe and our subconscious mind hear is "poor", thus bringing even more poverty your way. They become a part of psyche and drive you into taking action in line with what you keep saying. Using crystals while saying your affirmations can enhance the power of these affirmations. They increase the positive vibrations attached to these powerful words, drive us closer to our goals.

4. **Focus with confidence** – We create what we give maximum energy and attention to. What you offer your energy has the power of growing leaps and bounds. That is the power of focused energy or vibrations. Keep focused on your goals and objectives and feel confident that everything you desire has the power to be manifested or materialized. Focus continuously on things you want to attract in your life. This is one of the most important aspects of the 7 Law of Attraction. It is extremely vital that we concentrate strongly during the conceptualizing phase. This should be done on a regular basis and must become a habit. Do this as often as possible to accomplish the desired results. Focus on the positive thoughts, words, energies, and visuals associated with manifesting your dreams. Use crystals while meditating, visualizing, stating your affirmations, and focusing on your goals to amplify the positive vibrations associated with these thoughts.

5. **Profound Belief** – If you've read the book, *Ask And It Is Given,* through Esther Abraham talks about a burning desire in vibrational escrow. She lays out a variety of ideas on manifesting what one truly desires. Keeping our beliefs high about what we truly desire to manifest using any of the methods explained above is the key to breathing life into our

goals or desires. When crystals with positive vibrations are used while setting manifestation intentions, it infuses life into the process.

It is vital to keep your faith high and have belief in the power of your dreams to march forward and manifest your life goals. Allow yourself to sincerely believe that you have everything you desire. Consistent focus on what you desire along with a profound belief that what you seek to create is already yours is the key to manifesting it. It is important that you keep faith and belief in bringing forward what you want to manifest in life. Let yourself believe that the thing you want is already manifested or yours. That it is already a part of your reality.

6. **Have an attitude of gratitude** – Having an attitude of gratitude is vital to the process of manifesting your desires. Pick a stone or crystal of your choice and keep it with you all the time to amplify the feeling of thankfulness. Take the stone out from your wallet or bag and keep thanking it multiple times throughout the day for your blessings. Feel a sense of gratitude and thankfulness each time each time you touch the stone or crystal. Let it be a symbolic force of the earth or universe towards which you are expressing thankfulness for all that you have. Be grateful for what you have and what you desire to manifest even before you have it. Having an attitude of gratitude can help you create miracles. Be grateful in advance, even before you've manifested what you want. Being grateful in advance is extremely powerful, one of the major elements involved in attracting manifestation. Feel an abundance of gratitude daily for the things you have. It strengthens the action to help attract things we haven't manifested yet.

7. **Manifestation** – The things we truly focus on and desire become our destiny. That is the essence of the Law of Attraction. We have built through every step of the 7 Laws of

Attraction. This is the stage where we have created the ultimate result. We have now attracted into our life what we truly desire. Use your crystals and power stones throughout the 7 stages of the Law of Attraction to increase the energy of your manifestation processes. Once you receive what you truly desire, be grateful towards it. If you have been utilizing the 7 Laws of Attraction and have already manifested what you desire, it is vital to be aware that towards the end, you need to revisit step six gratitude and express thankfulness for what you've manifested to manifest even more.

Chapter Ten: Crystal Rituals for Protecting Your Energy

As people, we've always been conditioned to care for other people over ourselves. For most of us, this can extend to larger social circles like helping a friend in trouble. We are constantly hit by favors and requests to do things for other people throughout the day. This can drain our energy systems. The constant energetic firing can take a toll on our positive vibrations. Although we realize that this isn't good for us, and though we realize that we have been consciously or subconsciously impacted to adopt these habits, it can be challenging to refuse extending help. We don't want to say a no. People pour their hearts to us and we lend them a listening ear. They share all their problems with us and we often take on these problems as our own. This becomes even more marked in case of empaths and highly sensitive people. They tend to take on the energies of other people around them. This leaves them feeling drained and depleted. How does one protect one's energy in such a scenario?

To help maintain boundaries and protect one's own energy, work with a crystal to develop a protection ritual until you obtain the strength come back and your vibrations increase. Here is one such protection ritual that can be used when you are feeling more vulnerable.

Pick your protection crystal

When performing a protection ritual, pick a protection crystal you feel deeply connected with. Use a crystal that resonates with you along with one that possesses protection properties. Most crystals emit several properties but go with one that is known for its protection characteristic. It leads to more effective energy healing. Some of the most popular protection stones are amethyst, black tourmaline, black quartz, tiger's eye, smoky quartz, hematite, and obsidian. Obsidian is a highly potent stone and should be used with care. If you are experiencing feelings of emotional fragility, sensitivity, or being out of control, this may not be the best option as it brings to fore uncomfortable feelings.

Next, program your stone for protection. Keep a recently cleansed protection crystal in between your palms in a prayer position and shut the eyes. Visualize the stone being infused with pink light and start saying, "I devote this crystal towards the cause of protecting me." As you keep repeating this mantra, visualize the crystal being filled with pink light completely.

Keep the crystal with you through the day. It can be safely kept in your pocket, in your clothes or a bag, worn as jewelry and more. While keeping the stone in your bag is a great idea, during protection rituals, it is best to wear the stone on your body. Its vibrations should be felt by your being. In protection rituals, it is important to feel the energy of the stone on your person. The longer this crystal is on your person or the more you use it, the higher are your chances of influencing your energies. So wear the stone as much as you can to enjoy its optimal benefits.

Ensure you cleanse the stone daily. At the end of each day, charge and cleanse your stone to get rid of all the accumulated negative energy that was either being blocked or absorbed through the day with the crystal's healing properties. It is vital to cleanse your stone as part of a daily ritual since protection crystals tend to collect energetic build-up due to our tendency of almost always under an energetic attack. Some crystals are water soluble or sensitive to light and can experience wear and tear through various cleansing methods. Follow any of the cleansing methods mentioned in this book. Pick a cleansing ritual that seems right to you because at the end the day, you are cleaning your energy.

Hold the stone in your palms and visualize it being filled entirely with pink light. Push out all negativity. Allow the stone to be filled with light. Practice this until you absorb lower energy. If you have a Reiki level from 1-4, you may also use Reiki stones that carry symbols between your palms. Sound singing bowls or gongs, chant, sing, say "om" or "ah" to the crystals to release cleansing vibrations that cleanse stones. Instruments that release the sound waves also work well. Pass the crystal through the sound wave for eliminating impurities.

Ensure your crystal is protecting you all the time and tuning in to your vibrations. Keep the stone near your bedside or under your pillow while sleeping. When you awaken, grab the stone and wear it right away. Practice this protection ritual during a particularly vulnerable or challenging time or even when you are feeling energetically drained. Work on your protection stone each day until you feel your energy levels have risen to a position of control and strength.

A crystal ritual for new beginnings

This is a crystal ritual for new beginnings and can be performed with just about any healing crystals. The sacred ritual will not just help you kick start new things but also infuse the required doses of positivity into it.

Start by placing the crystal in your non-dominant hand. Shut your eyes like you are meditating or practicing visualization. Spend a few moments in releasing the negative thoughts held in your mind. Visualize an egg. Eggs represent new beginnings in Easter. Visualize or imagine an egg and picture yourself standing in the middle.

Urge the universe to lead you to the next beginning. When you visualize it, open your eyes and mention the new beginning. Now, take a pen and paper and mention the three things that are needed to accomplish your goal. Place your healing stone or crystal over this list. Place it somewhere where it can be easily spotted throughout the day.

The letting go ritual

Many times, past emotional baggage blocks our energy and prevents us from successfully marching into the future. This ritual helps us clear negative influences in life so we can move ahead with greater positivity and self-assurance. Think carefully about the negative forces you seek to eliminate from your life. Identify the things that are holding you back or acting as obstacles when it comes to leading a rewarding and fulfilling life. Negative folks, destructive relationships, or negative jobs? Recognizing the negative is the first step towards marching into a more positive and brighter future. Where is your toxic energy leading you? Are you able to live a life of your dreams or manifest what you seek with this toxic energy holding you back?

This goodbye ritual helps you clear any potentially negative influences in your life. You will bid farewell to all the unhealthy things that are holding your back. Name the things that are holding you back. Use selenite block or other forms of selenite crystal. Selenites are the most popular crystals when it comes to releasing unwanted elements from the past. Though selenite is the most popular crystal when it comes to 'let go' rituals, you can use any crystal of your choice that you can connect with a deeper, more spiritual level. Utilize a crystal that you may not need for the next couple of weeks. Whatever the crystal is saying to you today in terms of letting go is the one that you need to utilize for the ritual.

Set the intention. Write down things that you want to eliminate from your life. It can be anything from a bad habit to a negative person to an abusive relationship – anything that is stopping you from leading a fulfilling life. Who do you want to bid farewell to? Next, block it. Put the paper above your crystal and place it in a sacred space. This can be anywhere from your bedroom to a window sill to a nightstand. Any place that feels safe, positive, and sacred! Leave the space undisturbed for two weeks. The crystal's energies may actively work to eliminate the negativity from your life within the next 2 weeks. You will feel more positive, charged, and energetic when the negative vibrations are absorbed by the healing crystal. Letting go becomes easier when the negative and detrimental energies are cleansed out of your life over a period of 14 days.

The relationship ritual

This is a fantastic ritual when it comes to establishing meaningful and fulfilling relationships. This ritual must be performed with a partner. You are seeking to form a stronger and more fulfilling relationship with your partner. Use rhodonite or jasper for this ritual. You can perform this ritual before your upcoming date night. It can lead to have a more romantic and emotionally intimate relationship. Set intentions. Every partner needs to pick one of each of two crystals. Now, sit across each other and place the crystal on your heart. Take a couple of deep breaths together. Now, determine with the help of each other what you really want from the relationship. Stay honest, show respect, and demonstrate appreciation for each other.

Take turns in sharing. One partner should hold their palm facing up. The person holding their palm facing up is the listener. The other person continues holding the crystal above their heart. The one holding the crystal above their heart is the speaker. This person begins their thoughts that are deeply ingrained in love. Their sentences start with "I feel." The only thing a listener can say is "I hear you." He/she cannot say anything else. Now swap tasks. The speaker becomes the listener and listener becomes speaker.

Perform the same actions with the crystals. Share your appreciation with each other. Now, the speaker will list three things about their partner that they truly appreciate or are thankful for. It can be the smallest things such as grabbing coffee for the other person on the way from work. The listening partner can only say, "thank you." Take turns performing this ritual. This can be done each time before going for a date night.

Sage burning ritual

This is a crystal cleansing ritual that is over and above the ordinary. With the sage burning ritual, you can set an intention with each of your crystals. Cleansing crystals also cleanse your own energy and spirit. Gather your crystals and begin burning the sage. Utilize sage over other crystals when it comes to setting intention for creating more purity in life while also eliminating negativity. Repeat this ritual with each crystal. Pick these crystals one after the other and tell each crystal what you seek from it. How do you want them to benefit you? What are the things you seek from each crystal? The sage burning sets intentions for conducting any crystal healing ritual of your choice. It isn't mandatory that this has to be done. However, it will empower your future crystal healing rituals.

Broken heart ritual

Who doesn't need a little bit of healing from a broken heart? We've all experienced this. However, pretty much like everything else, there is a ritual for the broken heart too. This is a slightly longer crystal ritual and may take about half an hour. Utilize rose quartz for performing this ritual, although obsidian can also be a powerful healing element for broken hearts.

Clear your schedule, space, and time. Your space needs to be neat, clean, and well-organized before performing this ritual. Open the windows and allow a fresh lease of natural light and air to enter your space. Allow the sage to waft in the room while performing this ritual. Cleanse the stone thoroughly before using it for performing the ritual. Hold it in your hands and energize or program it for healing your heart. Ask it to do what you want. Say something such as, "I urge this crystal to clean my heart from negativity, damage, and pain. Empower me to experience the love I am looking for. Empower me to stay in love. I forgive myself for all the things that I've done in the past to bring pain, destruction, and negativity in the past. I forgive all energy that doesn't serve any purpose in my life anymore." Keep repeating the intention until you internalize and start feeling better. It is challenging. It won't happen immediately. Do it for as long as you feel comfortable. There's no time limit.

Beauty and love rituals

When it comes to beauty, romance, and love, Venus is the ruling planet. When it comes to crystals, Venus' favorite is rose quartz. There is no better crystal when it comes to performing healing and love rituals than rose quartz. It is a simple and effective ritual that doesn't have several functions tied into one. This is about attracting more love and beauty in your life. Step ahead and energize your rose quartz. Let us begin.

Rose quartz for more beauty! The first thing we do is place all our rose quartz stones on a big plate. Later, place your favorite beauty product on the plate. Keep aside the plate with your favorite beauty product and the rose quartz. The beauty products will gather love, energy, and light from your rose quartz and will supercharge your beauty the next time you apply make-up. If you have rose quartz essence or essential rose oil, infuse it on a spritzer and spritz the face before applying make-up. This is a loving, healing, and wonderful ritual.

If you have sufficient rose quartz stones for creating a platter, gather them on a plate once more. Place the rose quartz stones plate on an altar. This can be anything from a tiny table to a nightstand to a huge shelf. Just place it somewhere where it can be easily spotted. Each time you pass by, remind yourself about how gorgeous you are. Love will invariably flow to you.

The miracle manifesting ritual

Use this ritual to manifest miracles. One of the best crystals when it comes to manifesting miracles is tiger's eye. Even citrine works wonders when it comes to driving miracles. The more of these crystals you have, the better it is. Ensure your miracles are sufficiently charged. This may just help you manifest some of the best things in life. Gather all your tiger's eye or citrine stones. Place them on a plate similar to a compass. There have to be north, south, east, and west directions. This is done because four happens to be the foundations' number.

Now, determine what miracles you seek in life. Mention it aloud. You don't want to seek far-fetched miracles such as winning the lottery. That's a far-fetched wish at any given point of time. This is a serious ritual though. What do you truly want in life? You don't want something as unrealistic as prince charming knocking on your door? It helps to be realistic and set more practical, doable intentions. Leave your intentions grounded in the stone overnight under the moonlight. Fill your pockets with the stones next day and carry them with you for 10 days. Repeat this ritual each time you intended to manifest miracles.

Irrespective of the ritual you plan to perform, your rituals are yours. No one other than you owns them. They are not inscribed in stone. You can do whatever you are comfortable with. Your intentions are not written on the stone, they are in the stone. What do you want to manifest in life? It can be anything from healing a broken heart to a more loving relationship to more wealth to beauty. Use the power of these healing rituals to manifest whatever you seek in life. It will help attract more abundance and love into your life. Keep performing these rituals periodically to get into the habit of healing and cleansing your spirit.

Chapter Eleven: Quick Crystal Rituals

You don't need all the time in the world to work with crystals. A few quick, minute or two long rituals are enough to get you started in the right direction when it comes to using crystals for healing. Here are some quick ways you can work with these magnificent crystals when it comes to enhancing different aspects of your life.

Crystals are obviously gorgeous, filled with positive energy and the quickest way to help us transform our energies (unless there's a witch flying over you). They are one of the best healing and mysticism elements. Plus, working with a crystal's inherent properties can be fun. Whether your objective as a beginner is to create a large crystal grid or simply enjoy the beauty and vibrations of your stone, there are innumerable quick and easy rituals to connect with the energy of Mother Earth. Harness natural energy for healing and other purposes. Crystals are remarkable mechanisms of storing energy.

If you are new to crystals, the concept of ritual can be highly intimidating. Here's the real deal. Don't worry — you won't have witches flying around you on brooms. Here's the real deal. Rituals are a way to help us connect with our spirituality and mysticism in any form within our personal healing practices. They also do not have to be intense, elaborate, fancy, and time-consuming. You can perform quick, simple, and effective rituals to connect with the earth's energies and enhance different aspects of your life. Harness the magical energy of the earth to manifest your goals. Quick, easy, and effective rituals are awesome self-care practices that allow you to check-in with your deepest yourself. Think of this as a spiritual moment where you can connect with your deeper self in the middle of a busy life.

If you are a contemporary witch on the move, minute-long rituals will help you stay grounded without taking much of your time. Here are some rituals that can be performed quickly to give your self a mystical or spiritual energy boost. So, grab your crystals now and give them a go.

The creativity enhancing ritual

Creativity benefits several areas of our life – work, art, relationships, and even in building an Instagram grid. Utilizing crystals for healing facilitates opening of our creative channels to become more productive, inventive, and inspired.

Use carnelian - Carnelian is a powerful stone that stimulates the creative energy of our sacral chakra. It helps to awaken our creative side to infuse imagination, creativity, and inspiration in all aspects of our life.

Do this one minute ritual, hold the carnelian in your hand and state aloud, "I am a creative being." Words have amazing vibrations. By claiming our resourcefulness and creativity aloud, we amplify our positive vibrations. Amplify the mantra through your crystal to complete a fast and powerful ritual.

The love or relationship enhancing ritual

Use rose quartz – Who doesn't desire more love and fulfillment in their relationships? Using a rose quartz, one can connect with their kind heart chakra energy to manifest love for oneself but also everyone around you, including that special someone.

Rose quartz is the ideal crystal to use for this purpose. With its delicate pink hue, Rose quartz radiates compassionate and loving vibrations. You can perform several love rituals with the rose quartz since it stands for unconditional love and helps you connect with your heart chakra. Working with this opens us up to the love around us and the love we deserve from family, friends, and romantic makes. It is also connected to self-love. When we connect with our heart energy at a deeper level, we are able to experience greater love for ourselves and others.

Here's a quick one minute ritual for enhancing the love and romance in your life. Place the rose quartz crystal on your heart for a couple of minutes to connect with the love energy. Use these moments to establish a deeper connection with yourself. There is an energy exchange happening between you and the crystal. Connect with your own self-love. Feel the vibrations of love when you place the crystal on your heart. If you don't have it in you to love yourself, there's a slim chance you are going to love anyone else. Allow this crystal to help you love yourself before you go about loving others.

The motivation ritual

Use Jasper. If you need a motivational boost through a quick crystal ritual, jasper can work well. Red Jasper is balancing, grounding, and the perfect stone to help you get down to work. It has a positive and encouraging energy that offers you a feeling of being supported. Red Jasper helps us take action whether you are aiming to ace a new project or complete an existing one.

Here's a minute long ritual. Allow the stone to guide you towards areas that need a motivational shot. Ask yourself, what part of your life do you need to take action? Use red jasper for aligning your actions in line with the goal.

The health enhancing ritual

Use Blue apatite. Whether it is physical health, emotional balance, or changing habits/behavior patterns for the good, blue apatite can be highly effective when it comes to instilling us with willpower and motivation. Keeping this crystal is vital for helping us stay on track with our goals.

Blue apatite is a stunning blue stone that is perfect for letting you focus on your health goals. If you want to form more positive habits related to your health or let go of negative habit patterns, this is the ideal healing crystal. Since blue apatite governs our willpower, it inspires us to build healthy habits and governs our sense of willpower. The stone helps us sustain our motivation and keeps our willpower on track when it comes to accomplishing health and other goals.

Here's a one minute ritual you can practice with blue apatite. Hold your crystal and set a powerful and precise health intention. What is a health objective you want to accomplish? State the intention. Let the blue apatite offer you the willpower and motivation to accomplish your health goals. By stating your health intentions, you are infusing the stone with the right energy. Each time you see the stone or leave it within your living space, it'll remind you to make healthier and more mindful choices.

The wealth and prosperity enhancing ritual

Use pyrite. Pyrite is a bright and dazzling crystal that sparkles with the energy of wealth, prosperity, and abundance.

Here's a one minute ritual using pyrite. Place a pyrite crystal on your business card or anything that symbolized wealth creation endeavors. Place your company or employer's logo or a contract paper below the crystal. It can be a new gig that you are aiming to score as well. Some people prefer keeping it on top of a cash bundle to increase their wealth energy. Preferably, keep the crystal within your workspace for more energy.

The energy enhancing ritual

Use blue lace agate. When you feel out of shape owing to stress and do not have the time/money to accomplish your goals, try this minute-long stress relief ritual that helps you eliminate some steam naturally and effectively to develop a more relaxed and zen-like demeanor. Blue agate has a highly calming color. It helps release stress and keeps us calm and grounded. Its soothing, calming, and relaxing energy helps get rid of anxiety and stress. If you are feeling particularly low on energy or exhausted, the stone can help get you into a state of calmness.

Here's a one minute ritual using blue lace agate. Place the crystal in both hands (one at a time) to experience it's soothing, healing, and stress relieving vibrations. It guides us into a calmer and more relaxed state of being. Focus on the calming vibrations of the crystal. Visualize it spreading relief throughout your body and being, starting with your palms.

Enhancing clarity ritual

There is so much happening in our life all the time that it becomes challenging to focus on what one truly wants. We are unable to focus on or gain clarity about what we truly want. This prolongs the process of getting what we want. This simple and effective crystal ritual serves as a good starting point for using the healing energies of crystal to attain more clarity and focus in your endeavors. Clear quartz is ideal for clarity, given its own crystal clear characteristics. It offers mental clarity and illumination. It offers you the light to realize to know what you truly seek from life. Thus, if you are struggling to know what you truly want in life or are surrounded by too many things that are making it challenging to you to focus on important goals, crystal quartz is a wonderful stone to work with. Crystal quartz not just helps us determine what we want but also guides in the direction of going out there and fulfilling it.

How to use clear quartz for gaining greater clarity and freedom from chaotic thoughts crowding our mind? Meditate with your clear quartz for a couple of minutes to inspire its clarity. Let the clarity of this strong energy amplifying crystal lead you to do precisely what you need to do for accomplishing your goals.

The relaxation enhancing ritual

Use black tourmaline. Back home after a tiring day at work? Tired after a particularly exhausting social gathering? This means it is time to relax. Allow the magnificence of healing crystals to switch off your brain and slip into relaxation mode. You can throw in more relaxing treatments (bubble bath and other pampering treatments).

Black tourmaline is the king of all protection crystals. Black tourmaline forms a protective shield around you. This shield prevents you from gathering negative and unwanted energy from people and situations.

Here's a one minute energy protection ritual. Keep the black tourmaline crystal just outside your entrance door to offer a protective shield for your house along with those inside the space. Keep a black tourmaline just inside your entrance doorway to prevent unwanted energies from entering your space. Where ever you keep the crystal, visualize it building an energy shield. This seals off a space as well as your person from external negative energies! You may be coping with some bothersome energy suckers or vampires at work or suspect that your closest friend is actually a frenemy trying to harm you. In any event, calling on your crystal for spiritual protection isn't a bad idea. It is easy to perform a ritual.

The sleep enhancing ritual

Use celestite. Celestite is a surreal, dreamy crystal that has a calming effect that makes it an ideal stone for sleep time rituals.

No one desires to wake up foggy-eyed with lack of sleep, energy, and focus. Use your crystals to lull you into a feeling of sleepiness instead of trying to go scroll down your phone screen. Grab your most soothing and dreamiest crystal for this speedy night ritual to transport you into a serene dreamland in a mystical manner.

Celestite is a calming crystal that is ideal for attracting sleep time. The stone envelopes your space with relaxing and calming vibes to release anything that can hold you back from enjoying a good night's sleep.

Here is the ritual to help you sleep more peacefully. Before going to bed, place your celestite stone in your hands for experiencing a feeling of calmness and tranquility. When you are operating with disturbed energies, it is challenging to enjoy a peaceful sleep. State your intention of wanting to sleep peacefully aloud. Say, "I sleep in a calm and relaxing state" while holding the crystal in your hand. Put in your nightstand once you are done and go off into a deep, relaxed state.

Cultivating Head to Toe Chakra Healing with Crystals

That crystals are a miraculous healer is a well-known fact by now. The ability of chakra crystals as well as gemstones when it comes to balancing and harmonizing the body is tremendous. They won't just heal the body but also mind and spirit. Your body, mind, and spirit will feel completely rejuvenated. With crystals, you tap into the spirit of nature, which is known to have limitless potential. You will have several naturally wonderful and restorative tools each time you experience lack of focus, dis-balance, stressed and overwhelmed.

There is another ritual here that can heal you and energize your chakras. Laying on crystals or stones has been around for several thousand years. This involves keeping stones on different points of our body corresponding to specific chakras or the body's energy centers. This is referred to as balancing, clearing, or opening chakras. It eliminates stress from the body and makes us feel more cleansed, rejuvenated, and balanced. Balancing our chakras by laying stones not just keeps our blood and energy flowing through the body but also infuses the body with the required energy from gemstones, supporting our natural healing. This ritual that is still popular dates back to ancient teachings of Indian Vedic texts drafted several thousand years ago. In the present day, healers use chakra crystals for relieving stress, especially during the era of change. Enhance yourself self-esteem and sense of self-confidence, improve concentration, assist in creativity and person growth, promote inner peace, foster balance and harmony, and more.

If you are undergoing particularly trying emotional times, this crystal healing can be highly beneficial. When we are pained, we tend to go out of balance or feel slightly off center. Your heart chakra energy may be low or you may experience a feeling of being completely dis-balanced. There is a tendency to be low of physical, mental, and spiritual energy. When your heart or for that matter any energy chakra energy is running low, it can affect other areas of your life. There won't be any thought free flow or ideas related to forming health, mental, and spiritual connection. Some people respond very well to rose quartz placed on their heart chakra.

If you've experienced a particularly devastating event recently or simply seek some quiet time or balance for yourself, here is the ritual. Set a clear intention with your crystals. What is that you desire to accomplish through them? After setting the intention, allow the heart to open. This can be repeated multiple times. Place rose quartz or green malachite your heart chakra. Imagine your heart expanding and making greater room for love, joy, healing, and acceptance. Once you let go, you will experience a subtle yet powerful energy surge around your heart from the chakra crystal that has blanketed you with its warmth. It has now expanded like the sun's magnificent rays. After a while, you will experience a sense of peace and the heart's heaviness will evaporate. This is another wonderful ritual for emotional healing. As with any healing energy ritual, it is important to have the appropriate tools in hand. In this particular healing ritual, gemstones and chakra crystals are the keys. Using the power of these stones, you won't just heal your chakras or energy centers but also bring about a sense of balance in your physical, mental, and spiritual forces.

Much like any successful opening or healing, the right tools can make all the difference in the success of your ritual. In this particular case, chakra crystals and stones are the keys to unlocking your body, mind, and spirit's healing powers. Arranging the stones is easy. You place them on top of each other or specific stones on chakras that the stones correspond with. If not on the exact chakra, you can place them in the vicinity of the chakra. Leave the chakras there for a while to facilitate opening of the specific chakra. It is a simple yet highly effective ritual for circulating stagnant energy. If you do are unable to experience movement, tiny clear quartz positioned strategically on your body can facilitate and increase the energy of other stones.

You will feel your chakras open one after another after a single clearing session. Your energy may have become stagnant for months or years. Facilitating the circulation of energy that has been stagnant for years is a gradual process. Similar to exercise, you have to keep utilizing these crystals to view and feel the alterations in energy flow. These can be subtle at times. The changes are not always visible, but your body may take time to adapt to it over a period of time. How long should the stones be left on various chakras or energy centers of your body? Though there is no limit to the amount of time you must practice this ritual, you should do it for as long as you are comfortable doing it, keeping aside fifteen to twenty-five minutes works. Leaving the stones longer also works.

If you experience a feeling of discomfort at any point in time, remove the crystal or stone from the energy center. At times, your energy chakras may not respond favorably to their energy. The centers may end up feeling overwhelmed or uncomfortable. In such a scenario, try later. After the initial week, during which time you will gradually start laying one crystal every day on its corresponding energy chakra point. Aim for three sessions per week. Remember, cleansing out negative residue from mental, physical, emotional, and spiritual energy imbalances that may lead to constructive opportunities professionally, personally, and spiritually. The time you invest in yourself can yield rich results in terms of aligning your energies.

Chapter Twelve: Crystals and Gemstones for the 7 Chakras

Each chakra is closely associated with a specific body region and a specific region. Every chakra has its own role in optimizing a person's physical and mental health and overall well-being.

1. Root or Base Chakra

The root or base represents the feeling of staying grounded and passionate. Its primary color is red. Where is it located? The chakra is located in the base of our spine. When this particular chakra is weak, exhausted, dis-balanced and stressed, we experience lower back or leg pain. There are other immune system disorders too. One needs to get into survival mode. When the same chakra is open, a person feels at ease in his/her body. The person feels empowered and filled with life. Put a red crystal between the thighs, near your groin. Visualize the color red with all its warmth and splendor. It represents our foundation, family, and passion. What are the recommended chakra stones? Some of the recommended chakra stones are ruby, jasper, and bloodstone. Use these stones to open your root chakra and bring about a sense of harmony and well-being within your physical, mental, and spiritual forces.

2. Sacral Chakra

The sacral chakra represents creativity and the ability to accept other people. Sacral chakra's predominant color is orange. It is located two inches above the navel. You may feel a sense of confusion, overdependence on other people, frustration, and lack of motivation when it's low. A person may experience swelling or low hormonal levels. On the other hand, when one's sacral chakra is open, it leads to a feeling of flexibility in the mind and body. There is greater creativity, playfulness, and openness. Opening of the sacral chakra signifies resourcefulness, inventiveness, and ideas. To heal this chakra, place a healing orange stone over the pelvic bone. Visualize the color orange and see yourself as a creative individual. The recommended chakra stones are carnelian, orange aventurine, dark citrine, orange calcite, and tangerine quartz.

3. Solar Plexus

The solar plexus region is associated with our intellect and how we perceive the world around us. Its primary color is yellow. The solar plexus is located in our upper abdomen.

What happens when the energy of the solar plexus is low? When the solar plexus energy is low, we feel a lack of control, greater fearfulness, low self-confidence or an inherent inability to experience emotions. We may also experience some digestion problems. This area is particularly connected with a feeling of lack of worthiness when its energy is running low. In addition to this, there are other physiological problems as well.

When the solar plexus region is open, a person may experience a feeling of being free from the need to constantly control things. A person is likelier to be more open to new ideas, creativity, innovation, and resourcefulness. There is an inherent need to be flexible towards suggestions, happiness, feelings, and joy. A person also experiences efficient digestion. Keep a yellow crystal a couple of inches above the belly button. Think of the color yellow or a bright and dazzling sunny day. Keep in mind your power center and the ability to manifest.

The recommended chakra stones to open the solar plexus chakra include citrine and amber.

4. The Heart Chakra

Our heart chakra represents the body and our ability to love unconditionally while also accepting others. The color associated with our heart chakra is green. It is located at the center of the chest. When the heart chakra is low, we may feel exhausted, stressed, bitter, jealous, and anxious. A person may also experience low or high blood pressure. His/her heart rate may become abnormally high or low when the energy is running low. There may also be lumps or cysts in the breasts.

When the heart chakra is open, you may experience a greater sense of relaxation, acceptance, openness to new relationships, and the ability to sustain more harmonious and balanced relationships. You may experience a greater sense of forgiveness, joy, and love.

Place a pink or green stone on the breastbone. Visualize various colors such as green and pink. Think of mending, harmonizing, and soothing ways to open the heart. Rose quartz is known to be especially effective when it comes to nurturing, balancing, and soothing the heart's emotional centers. Think of this green as soothing, calming, and healing our heart. Release anger and other negative emotions. There is no space for any negativity in your heart. Open it and allow it to embrace the positives. Let your heart be open to receiving all the good things that it deserves.

What are some of the recommended chakra stones? Some of the recommended chakra stones include malachite, green moss, emerald, rose quartz, rhodochrosite, tourmaline, green tourmaline, agate, aventurine, and watermelon tourmaline.

5. The Throat Chakra

The throat chakra represents communication, articulation, and self-expression. It is associated with the color blue and is located in the throat. When the energy is running low, you may experience feelings of isolation, being misunderstood, and stuttering. Low throat energy can also lead to a sore throat, stiff neck, and a tight jaw.

When the throat energy is open, you may experience a greater sense of expression, communication, and articulation. You will have healthier, gums, teeth, mouth, and nasal passages. You can position a blue crystal on your larynx. Visualize the color blue deeply. Think of articulate communication, positive speech, and word power. Some recommended chakra stones include lapis lazuli, turquoise, blue sapphire, aquamarine, and sodalite.

6. Third Eye or Brow Chakra

The third eye or brow represents understanding, comprehension, and the power to focus. It also represents intuition and keeping our eyes firmly fixated on the bigger picture. The color representing our third eye chakra is indigo. It is located on the forehead between our eyes. When the third eye or brow chakra is running low, we may experience an overactive mind, inflexibility, foggy brain, and stiff neck.

On the other hand, when the third eye chakra is open, a person may experience greater clarity of mind, an enhanced ability to solve problems, higher intuition, the ability to comprehend matter more easily, and focus. Place a purple stone between your brows or the Third Eye, which is known to be a highly calming spot. Deeply visualize purple color. Focus on intuition and clarity.

What are the recommended chakra stones for your throat chakra? Lapis, iolite, and amethyst!

7. The Crown Chakra

Our crown chakra stands for divine inspiration. Its predominant color is violet. It is located on top of one's head. What happens when your crown chakra energy is running low? For starters, you may experience feelings of clumsiness, lack of inspiration, lack of certainty, a feeling of being out of step with reality, uncertain of your identity and purpose in life, and rigidity in thinking.

What happens when the crown chakra is open? When our crown chakra is open, we experience feelings of greater flexibility, understanding life's flow, the ability to remain unshaken by setbacks, gain greater clarity, and develop the ability to perceive things like they are. Place a violet crystal above your head. Visualize a white light. Think of a strong connection with the divine. The recommended chakra stones are light amethyst and clear quartz.

Conclusion

Thank you again for downloading this book.

I sincerely hope that this book was able to give you comprehensive, actionable, straightforward, and proven ways to use crystals for improving your physical, mental, and spiritual health.

The next step is to act by following all the simple yet highly effective rituals and guidelines mentioned in the book for making the most of your crystals. Identify rituals that work for you and that you can connect with at a higher level and follow it in a disciplined, regulated, and consistent manner.

Practice the techniques described in the book for accomplishing greater focus, clarity, goal manifestation, physical health, wealth, and more. Begin with the easier sessions, and let it grow into a more extensive practice.

Begin today, for a person who gains knowledge without implementing it, is not any better than a person who cannot read. Knowledge is futile if not applied.

Lastly, if you enjoyed reading the book, please take the time to share your thoughts by posting a review. It'd be greatly appreciated!

Here's to the power of your crystals!

www.ingramcontent.com/pod-product-compliance
Lightning Source LLC
Chambersburg PA
CBHW070048230426
43661CB00005B/817